Grades 3-6

Teaching Career Essentials

HELPING CHILDREN LEARN CRITICAL INSIGHTS & SKILLS

By Lisa King, Ed.S.

© 2015 by YouthLight, Inc. | Chapin, SC 29036

All rights reserved. Permission is given for individuals to reproduce the worksheets in this book. Reproduction of any other material is strictly prohibited.

Layout and Design by Melody Taylor/GraphicSolutions, Inc.
Project Editing by Susan Bowman

ISBN: 978-1-59850-164-3
Library of Congress Control Number: 2014946791

10 9 8 7 6 5 4 3 2 1
Printed in the United States

Acknowledgements:

I would like to acknowledge the following people who have helped me in my career, in my life, and with this book:

- My parents who I am so blessed to have as guides through life and in adulthood as friends.
- My husband and daughter for love, patience, support and everything and beyond.
- My sister and sister/friends for knowing me sometimes better than I know myself.
- My counselor friends, colleagues, and supervisors in Cobb County School System who are amazing listeners, inspiring professionals, and forward-thinking advocates.
- My family at Blackwell Elementary who make work feel like a home away from home.
- Susan and Bob Bowman for your edits, ideas, and having confidence in me.

Dedication:

I would like to dedicate this book to my husband and daughter, Bryan and Grace. I can grow in my career because of the love, patience, and support. You both are indeed "essential" to me, and I love you to the moon and outer space.

Table of Contents

Introduction 5
Overview of Career Clusters 6
Teacher Needs Assessments.. 7
Teacher and Student Questionnaires 8
School and Career Connection Posters 9
Make the Connection Paper Clip Trick 12
Connecting to Careers: Skills for Success 13

Chapter 1:	**Career Exploration**	**14**
Activity 1.0	Literature Link	15
Activity 1.1	Career Connection Card	17
Activity 1.2	Career Maze..	18
Activity 1.3	Word Search and Crossword	19
Activity 1.4	Career Cluster Collage...	21
Activity 1.5	Career Magic Square	22
Activity 1.6	Today vs. Someday Career Exploration......................................	24
Activity 1.7	Compare and Contrast Careers	27
Activity 1.8	Roll a Question	28
Activity 1.9	Snowmen at Work	29
Activity 1.10	How on Earth Do You Get a Job?	33
Activity 1.11	Career Awareness Secret Message	36
Activity 1.12	Career Sundaes	40
Activity 1.13	Career Wax Museum	42
Activity 1.14	Career Family/Community Tree...	45
Activity 1.15	Career Connections with School Subjects	47
Activity 1.16	Career Inventory..	48
Activity 1.17	Cocoa Bean to Chocolate Showdown	49
Activity 1.18	Career Day Reflection	51
Activity 1.19	Creating a Local Database of Speakers for your School	53
Activity 1.20	Career Centers...	54
Chapter 2:	**Work Ethic**	**55**
Activity 2.0	Literature Link	56
Activity 2.1	Counselor Connection Card	58
Activity 2.2	What is Work Ethic Poem	59
Activity 2.3	Cryptogram	60
Activity 2.4	Do Your Best Story / Make and Take Magnet	61
Activity 2.5	Making your Mark: What is Work Ethic?	66

Activity 2.6	Roll a Question	67
Activity 2.7	Work Ethic Poster	68
Activity 2.8	Good to Great	69
Activity 2.9	Step 1,2, 3 Goal: Build a Snowman	70
Activity 2.10	Famous Failures	72

Chapter 3: Self-Control 75

Activity 3.0	Literature Link	76
Activity 3.1	Counselor Connection Card	77
Activity 3.2	Word Jumble	78
Activity 3.3	On the Job Self-Control Role Plays	79
Activity 3.4	Coffee Filter Thoughts	81
Activity 3.5	Gimme 5 ways of Deep Breathing	84
Activity 3.6	Circle of Control	86
Activity 3.7	Stop and Think Willow	88
Activity 3.8	Self-Control Dough	91
Activity 3.9	'Just Right' Meter	92
Activity 3.10	Teacher Pre post for small group	94

Chapter 4: Teamwork 95

Activity 4.0	Literature Link	96
Activity 4.1	Counselor Connection Card	98
Activity 4.2	Teamwork Poem	99
Activity 4.3	Teamwork Cryptogram Activity	101
Activity 4.4	Don't Lose Your Marbles Teamwork Game	106
Activity 4.5	Play Dough a la Teamwork	107
Activity 4.6	Career Cluster Showdown	109
Activity 4.7	Teamwork: Being a Piece of the Puzzle	111
Activity 4.8	Crayon Box Activity	116

Chapter 5: Organization 118

Activity 5.0	Literature Link	119
Activity 5.1	Counselor Connection Card	120
Activity 5.2	Poem	121
Activity 5.3	Word Search	122
Activity 5.4	Story Connection: Clutter Buster and the Desk Fairy	123
Activity 5.5	Organization Numbers Game... You Gotta Have a Plan	126
Activity 5.6	Organization Relay	128
Activity 5.7	Excellence vs. Organization	130
Activity 5.8	STAR Students (Students Taking Academics Responsibly)	132
Activity 5.9	Organization Centers	133
Activity 5.10	Froggy Gets Dressed: Do Things in Order	137

Condensed Bibliotherapy List 139

Introduction

The Structure of the Curriculum

When the ASCA Model was established in 2005, it gave counselors a structure on how to create a comprehensive developmental counseling program. As we all got used to the person/social, career and academic domains being the mainstay of our curriculum, it quickly became clear that there was a lack of resources at the elementary level.

The first chapter of this book addresses Career Exploration and has many lessons that can be done in preparation or in conjunction with Career Day. The subsequent chapters support "soft skills" or topics that are important to be a good student or to be a good employee. These are the skills that will connect children to their future careers. These lessons, puzzles, ideas, posters, and activities are kid-tested and kid-approved and hopefully will help counselors add to their programs.

How to Use this Book with Classroom Guidance and Small Groups

Whether in classroom guidance or in small group sessions, this book can serve as a guide to counselors. One way to make a comprehensive program consistent within a school is to teach lessons that cover the ASCA standards and also cover similar lessons year to year, expanding upon the content covered in previous years. As shown below, making a simple excel spreadsheet of lessons covered can help counselors remember what topics were covered in years past.

Sample of Annual Overview/Outline

	Self-Control	Organization	Work Ethic	Teamwork
2nd grade	Willow Can't Wait	Froggy	Do Your Best Magnets	Crayon Box
3rd grade	Mouth is a Volcano	Desk Fairy	Posters	Puzzle Pieces
4th grade	Hocus Focus Game	Relay Lesson	Make Your Mark	Don't Lose Marbles
5th grade	Coffee Filter	Org. Centers	Famous Failures	Cryptograms

The Push to Teach about Career Clusters in Elementary Schools

In 2005 when the ASCA National Model was created, school counselors came to understand how to implement the three domains (personal/social, academic, and career) into their practice. At about the time counselors got used to implementing career lessons into their programs, there was a push to teach about the 16 career clusters at the elementary level. Career has always been the trickiest domain to implement due to the developmental nature of elementary students. Elementary counselors have stepped up to be creative in this pursuit and my hope is that this book will assist in inspiring counselors to continue teaching in creative ways about careers, about the skills needed to be successful, and about the introduction of career clusters. (See Career Cluster Overview on page 6).

Overview of Career Clusters

From The Department of Education

Career Cluster	Explanation	Jobs within this cluster
Agricultural & Natural Resources	Careers in processing resources including food, wood products, natural resources, and other plant and animal products.	Farmer, Marine Biologist, Environmental Design, Water Plant Operator
Health Science	Careers in diagnosing and treating injuries and illnesses as well as health support services including research.	Paramedic, Doctor, Nurse, Veterinarian, Speech Pathologist, Pharmacist,
Architecture & Construction	Careers in planning, managing, building and maintaining the built environment.	Brickmason, Architect, Contractor, Roofer, Plumber
Arts, A/V Technology & Communications	Careers in performing, writing, publishing, journalism, and entertainment services that might include behind the scenes to make a performance successful.	Actors. News Reporters, Photographer, Editors, Radio Announcer, Fashion Designer.
Business & Administration	Careers that organize, direct and evaluate functions essential to running a business.	Accountants, Office Managers, Clerks, Executive, Supervisor
Education & Training	Careers that promote education such as teaching/training, and professional support services.	Teacher, Coach, Corporate Trainer, Professor, Librarian
Finance	Careers in financial and investment planning, banking, insurance, and business management.	Accountant, Banker, Financial Planner, Insurance Sales
Government & Public Administration	Careers in planning and executing government functions at the local, state and federal levels and national security.	Mayor, Lawyer, Legislator, Judge, Court Reporter
Hospitality & Tourism	Careers related to restaurants and food/beverage services, hotels, travel and tourism.	Travel Agent, Hotel Employee, Tour Guide
Human Services	Careers that relate to families and human needs such as mental health services, and community services.	Teacher, Chef, Firefighter, Military, Waitress, School Counselor, Police Officer
Information Technology	Careers related to the design, development, and support of computer and software systems.	Computer Operator, Video Game Designer, Software Engineer, Website Developer
Law & Public Safety	Careers in public safety, protective services and homeland security	Firefighter, Police Officer, FBI, Security Guard
Manufacturing	Careers working with products and equipment including design and materials on things like cars, computers, appliances, airplanes, or electronic devices.	Factory Worker, Furniture Repairman, Machine Operator
Marketing and Advertising	Careers in research of brands, sales, merchandising, and marketing.	Commercial Writer, Billboard Designer
STEM	Careers in providing scientific research including laboratory and testing services.	Scientist, Mathematician, Engineer, Astronaut
Transportation, Distribution & Logistics	Careers in the movement of people and materials by road, air, rail and water and related services such as transportation infrastructure planning.	Bus Driver, Postal Worker, Pilot, Packaging Facilities, Air Traffic Control

Teacher Needs Assessment for Classroom Curriculum Lessons

What do you want me to teach in counselor curriculum lessons?

Grade Level _____

This year, my lessons will focus on teaching students the importance of being "Professional Students." These lessons will reinforce skills that you are already teaching in your classrooms. Below is a list of topics within the curriculum I will be teaching. I am interested in knowing specifically which skills you would like for me to address in my lessons.

Please number the topics 1-5 in the order in which you find these topics a priority (1 being most important to cover, 5 being less of a priority). Thank you for your input.

_____ Organization
_____ Career Exploration
_____ Work Ethic
_____ Teamwork
_____ Self-Control

Student Pre/Post Needs Assessment for Classroom Curriculum Lessons or Small Group

Teacher: Please fill out this questionnaire to help identify the strengths and weaknesses of your student's study skills. You will be given this again at the end of group to measure what skills this student has gained.

Student's Name _____ Today's date _____

For each statement, please rate the student:

	Strongly Agree	Agree	Disagree	Strongly Disagree
This student exhibits effective active listening skills.				
This student displays a strong work ethic.				
This student's desk is organized.				
This student turns in homework on time.				
This student completes class work.				
This student works well with a team.				
This student displays a positive attitude about learning.				
The student has good behavior in class.				

Student Questionnaire

Student's Name _____ Today's date _____

Please answer each statement. Remember there are no wrong answers.

	Strongly Agree	Agree	Disagree	Strongly Disagree
I am a good listener.				
I try to do my best with my school work.				
My desk is organized.				
I turn in homework on time.				
I complete my class work.				
I work well work with others.				
I have a good attitude about learning.				
I have good behavior in class.				

Making the Connection Posters

As school counselors, we are charged with helping students understand how the skills they learn in school will help them in their future. The skills counselors usually work on are what are sometimes called "soft skills." It is crucial that we use our platform as counselors to do some PR to help students visualize how these skills can help. The posters below can be replicated on a larger scale for bulletin boards, or as is for wall displays in or out of classrooms. There is an example of one way to display them below.

Help your students make the connection, by having them color the posters included (pages 10-11) and then create construction paper links that can be labeled with the skills that you are going to be emphasizing in your curriculum.

For instance if you are going to cover the skills in this book throughout the year, you could make separate construction paper links labeled WORK ETHIC, SELF-CONTROL, TEAMWORK, ORGANIZATION. If you have other topics you are going to cover, make a label on your display for that skill. (For more skill-based lessons see Making the Link by Lisa King (2005) for lessons on Listening Skills, Responsibility, Learning Styles, Time Management, Goal Setting, Testing Skills, and other Career Awareness lessons)

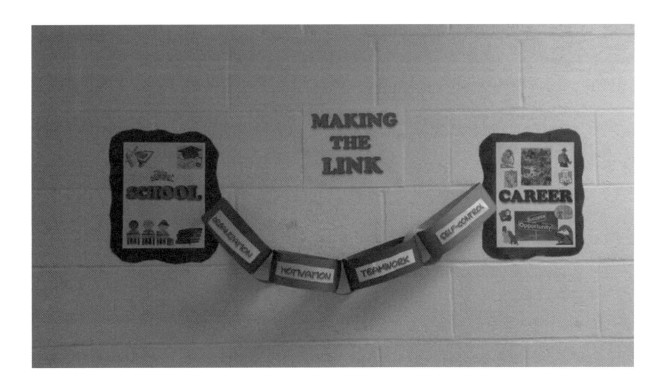

School

$E=mc^2$

school

Career

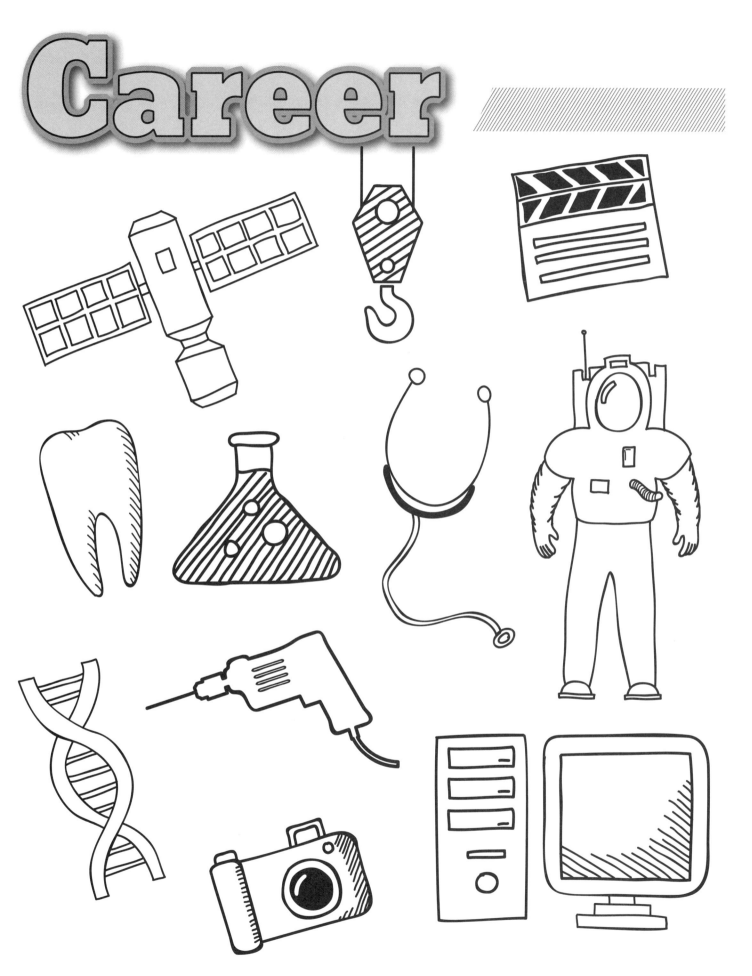

Worksheet: Making the Connection Paper Clip Trick

Materials: Paper strip or cut-out of the example below, 2 paper clips

Procedures:

1. Fold your paper into thirds (on the dotted line) so that one third is folded over the top, and the bottom third is folded underneath. If you look at this from the side it'll look like a Z.

2. Place the paper clips so that one paper clip is fastened on top (holding the 1st and 2nd thirds together) next to one end of the strip of paper. The second paper clip is fastened to the bottom (holding the 2nd and 3rd, thirds together) next to the other end of the paper strip. Each paper clip should only clip over two pieces of the paper strip.

3. Make sure you have about 1 inch of space between the paper clips, and there is enough of each end of the paper for you to grab onto. Hold the ends of the paper and gently begin to pull.

4. As you pull, the clips will get closer and closer together. Before they meet, give the paper a firm tug and the two paper clips will link together.

Habits Today		**Future Career**

Habits Today		**Future Career**

Habits Today		**Future Career**

Worksheet: Connecting To Careers: Skills for Success

Directions: Complete this worksheet to tell what you know about the following topics. This can be before you learn about these or after learning about these topics.

Name: _____

Where do you go to school?

What do you know about **SELF-CONTROL?**

What do you know about **ORGANIZATION?**

What do you know about **TEAMWORK?**

What do you know about **WORK ETHIC?**

What do you see yourself doing for a career in the future?

Chapter 1: Career Exploration

It matters not what someone was born, but what they grow to be. – Albus Dubmledore

ASCA Competencies addressed in this chapter:
- Learn about the variety of traditional and nontraditional occupations
- Demonstrate knowledge about the changing workplace
- Identify personal skills, interests and abilities and relate them to current career choice
- Demonstrate knowledge of the career-planning process
- Know the various ways in which occupations can be classified

Chapter Introduction
Students start to think about their future at a very young age. School counselors can help students explore a scope of different ideas that will help them hone in on their skills and interests and how these things help formulate possible career choices.

Activity	Page #	Chapter Contents
1.0	15	Literature Link
1.1	17	Career Connection Card
1.2	18	Career Maze
1.3	19	Word Search and Crossword
1.4	21	Career Cluster Collage
1.5	22	Career Magic Square
1.6	24	Today vs. Someday Career Exploration
1.7	27	Compare and Contrast Careers
1.8	28	Roll a Question
1.9	29	Snowmen at Work
1.10	33	How on Earth Do You Get a Job?
1.11	36	Career Awareness Secret Message
1.12	40	Career Sundaes
1.13	42	Career Wax Museum
1.14	45	Career Family/Community Tree
1.15	47	Career Connections with School Subjects
1.16	48	Career Inventory
1.17	49	Cocoa Bean to Chocolate Showdown
1.18	51	Career Day Reflection
1.19	53	Creating a Local Database of Speakers for your School
1.20	54	Career Centers

Activity 1.0 – Literature Link: Career Explorations

Below are books that will correlate with career exploration lessons. There is a line before each book so that you can mark where it is located, so that if you decide to use it in a lesson you know where to find it. (Personal Library, Media Center, online audiobook, Public Library, or Need to Order it)

_____ **Snowmen at Work by Carolyn Buehner** – While we sleep, snowmen play and also have careers. They are dentists, pizza delivery and factory workers who are all busy at work. (Lesson on page 29.)

_____ **Clothesline Clues To Jobs People Do by Kathryn Heling** – Clotheslines are shown and the narrator asks readers to guess the person who fits the descriptions. This is a fun way to introduce jobs in a fun kid-friendly way.

_____ **There by Marie Louise-Fitzpatrick** – A little girl with a bag keeps asking questions like, "When will I get there?" and "Will it take long to get there?" The future is a big question mark, and she wonders if it's safe to enter, if she'll be the same there, or will things be different. This is a great book for looking into the future and also for students transitioning to middle school.

_____ **Someday by Eileen Spinelli** – This book alternates between present tense and Someday. A little girl dreams of a career as an archaeologist, an animal scientist, and gymnast. On some pages she enjoys being a kid doing things she will need to reach her goals–digging, counting, cartwheels. It's fun to have students connect today with someday. (Lesson on page 24.)

_____ **These Hands by Margartet Mason** – Joseph's grandfather could do almost anything. He could play the piano, throw a ball, and tie a triple knot. But in the 1960s, he could not bake bread at a factory because of racism. Joseph learns that people joined together to fight discrimination so that one day, their hands could do anything in the world.

_____ ***Silly Lilly in What Will I Be Today*** – Each day, Lilly imagines herself in a different job. As most children do, Lilly believes she can be anything from a City Planner to a Ballerina. This book would make a great addition to an introduction to careers.

_____ ***Sally Gets a Job* by Stephen Huneck** – Sally is a curious dog and she wants a job. Sally thinks it's a good idea if she gets a job like everyone in her family. There are so many options to choose from. She likes digging in the yard, so maybe she could be an archaeologist and she likes playing ball, so maybe she could be a baseball player. She imagines a lot of different careers.

_____ ***How to Get a Job…by Me, the Boss (How To Series)* by Sally Lloyd-Jones** – The Boss might not even be out of first grade, but she definitely claims to know what she's talking about. She also has funny advice as to the jobs you can have when you grow up and how to get them. The most important advice the Boss has is to do something that you love and something you're good at.

_____ ***A New Job for Dilly* by Rena Jones** – This book is about a rat who tries different jobs from A to Z. Dilly loves pickles and wants a job so he doesn't have to swipe them from the deli like a thief. Will he ever find the perfect career?

_____ ***The Night Worker* by Kate Banks** – Every night, Papa goes off to work. He's an engineer at a construction site and a night worker. One night, Papa gives Alex his own hard hat and they go out into the night to Papa's busy job site full of street sweepers, delivery men, heavy machinery and cranes. As the day dawns, all is quiet and little Alex has gone to sleep, dreaming of being a night worker when he grows up.

_____ ***Big Plans* by Bob Shea** – A little boy plots his future, and he has big plans. This story is great for any child who is ready to dream big.

_____ ***Whose Tools are These?* by Katz Cooper** – This fun interactive book, is not the ordinary book about community workers and introduces the children to the tools used by community workers. Readers can explore work life in their communities with predictable text and fun facts

_____ ***Sid the Squid: and the Search for the Perfect Job* by David Derrick** – Sid decides that he wants to find the perfect job. He tries many different jobs, but each one has its own challenges but he finally finds a job that is a perfect fit.

_____ ***LMNO Peas* by Keith Baker** – Busy little peas explore different careers along with the letters of the alphabet. From Acrobat Peas to Zoologist Peas, this great picture book highlights different interests, hobbies, and careers each one paired with a letter of the alphabet.

_____ ***My Name is not Isabella* by Jennifere Fosberry** – A little girl imagines herself as some famous heroes from days past. This book is a great way to talk about dreams of making a difference in a career of your choice in the future.

_____ ***From Cocoa Bean to Chocolate (Start to Finish)* by Robin Nelson** – This book takes you through the process of making chocolate from the very beginning of the process. It is a great way to open a discussion about how many different careers lend a hand in creating products.

Activity 1.1 – Career: Counselor Connection Card

Directions: After a lesson on Career Exploration is taught, give each student a copy of the counselor connection card below. If they bring it back by a designated date, they are eligible to win a prize. You can draw three of the counselor connection cards that have been returned and those students are given a prize.

Counselor Connection Card

Student Name:_____ Date:_____ Teacher_____

Student: Interview a person who has a job. Ask the following questions and write the answers. After you complete this, turn it in to your counselor.

Person's Name:_____

Person's Job: _____

❯ What are other jobs you have had in your life? _____
_____
_____

❯ If you had choice, would you keep this job or would you do something different?
_____
_____

❯ What do you like about working? _____
_____

❯ What don't you like about working? _____
_____
_____

Activity 1.2 – Finding a Career is A-MAZE-ING

In real life the search for a career can feel like a crazy maze. Many people have many different careers in their lifetime. Can you try and help this person find their way to the future? Each time you pass a hat, think about whether or not you would want that job.

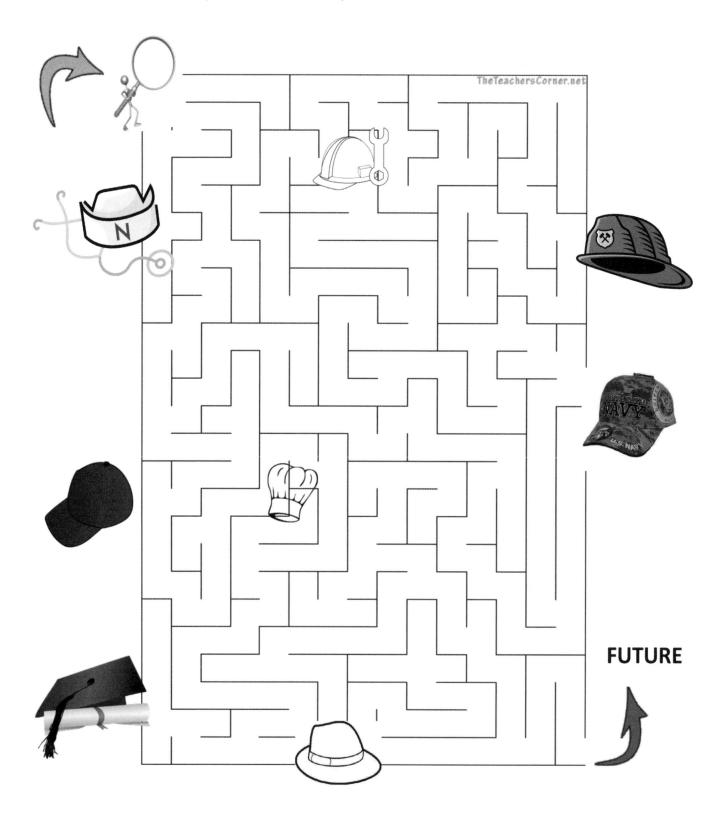

Activity 1.3a – Career Exploration

Make Your Own Word Search

Name of who created the puzzle _____

Directions: Enter 12 career titles into the template below horizontally, vertically, or diagonally, but not backwards. Then, fill in the rest of the boxes with random letters. As you write your careers into the puzzle, also write them into the word bank. Later, you will exchange papers with a friend, and have them complete your word search you created.

Word Bank:

_____   _____   _____

_____   _____   _____

_____   _____   _____

_____   _____   _____

Name of person who solved the puzzle _____

Activity 1.3b – Career Exploration

Words to Know for Career Awareness Name _____

Directions: Using the word bank below, solve this crossword puzzle with the words about career awareness.

Across
1. When you apply for a job and get it you are _____.
5. People who work with you
7. The person in charge at a job
8. When someone does not have a job, they are _____.
9. What someone is paid
10. If your boss thinks you are doing a great job, you might get more money which is called a _____.
11. When trying to start a new career, you might want to be an _____ to learn about it.

Down
2. A meeting where a boss asks you questions to decide if you will be hired.
3. Another word for a job
4. The education you need to do a job
6. Someone's education, work history, and qualifications on paper

WORD BANK:

| Interview | Hired | Resumé | Occupation | Intern | Unemployed |
| Salary | Boss | Raise | Coworker | Training | |

Activity 1.4 – Career Cluster Collages

Overview: Allow an art project to guide student learning about career clusters.

Materials: Paint, Doctor Supplies (cotton balls, band aids, gauze, etc.), Paper, Magazine Clippings (of doctors, and supplies)

Procedures:

1. Discuss that career clusters are organized into 16 broad categories that include almost all occupations from entry through professional level.

2. Either assign children to groups or allow them to choose. Groups are recommended for 3-4 students but more could be assigned if using poster board or large sheets of poster paper.

3. Give the children supply bags in large (2 gallon Ziploc bags) and let them create their own collage. Option (Have sample collages for each career cluster offered)

4. Use the guide below to create your collage supply bags.
    - Health Services: Doctor Supplies (Cotton Balls, band aids, gauze, etc.)
    - Hospitality & Tourism: Brochures from states, menus, hotels, national parks, etc.
    - Marketing: Magazines ads, brochures
    - Architecture and Construction: Craftsticks, pipe cleaners, blueprints
    - Transportation, Distribution & Logistics: Cutouts of vehicles and maps
    - Finance: Fake dollar bills and coins
    - Agriculture and Natural Resources: Recycled containers of food

Optional: Have students go to www.paws.bridges.com/cfnc1.htm and go to the Job Finder. Students can see which cluster they might be good at and create a collage for one or more of those.

Optional: Have Collages decorated with names of jobs within the cluster interspersed. Then, have a contest to see how many jobs within those clusters that the students can name.

Activity 1.5 – Career Magic Square

Overview: Students will examine career readiness skills through creating a hands-on game.

American School Counselor Association Indicator:
• Identify attitudes and behaviors, which lead to successful learning

Materials: Magic Square Worksheet page 23

Procedures:

1. Review test taking skills that the students have learned in years passed.

2. Distribute the career magic square on page 23.

3. Have students follow the directions and create their magic square. Allow students to pair up with a partner.

4. Tell students, "With your partner follow these directions with one person using their magic square first and the other one gets to be the "chooser." When you are using your magic square tell the chooser to:

    – Pick a number (then you count out that number and open and close the magic square for each number counted.

    – Then ask the chooser, "What is a career cluster that you might like to work in?"

    – Then uncover that flap with that career cluster and ask the chooser the question written there.

5. When each person in the pair has been the chooser you can have the class switch partners and repeat this activity.

Worksheet 1.5: Career Magic Square

Directions for how to make your career magic square:

1. Cut along the solid lines of the outer square.
2. With the writing facing down, fold each corner to the center.
3. Then, turn the paper over and fold the corners to the center again.
4. Fold the paper in half with the circle facing the outside.
5. Write different numbers of your choice (1-10) in each circle
6. With both hands, put your pointer finger and thumb under the paper flaps. The numbers within the circles are showing on the top.

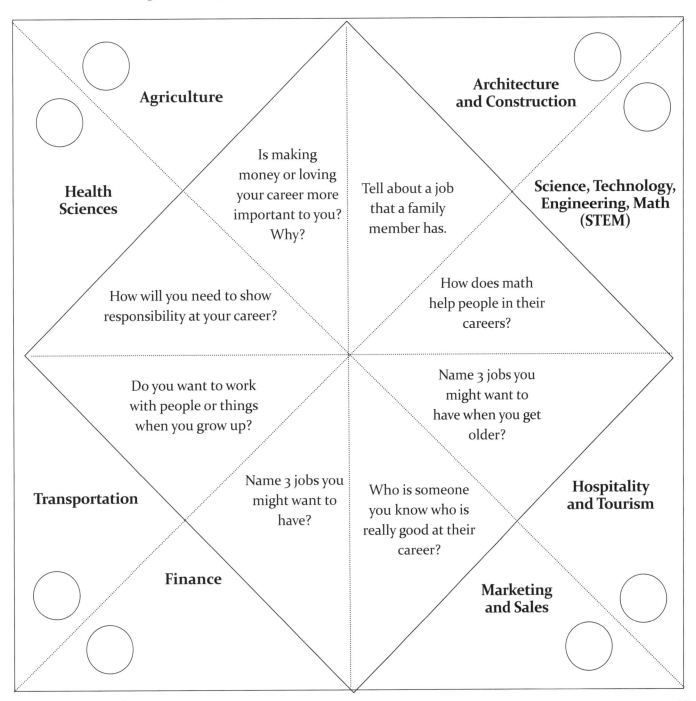

©YouthLight • 23

Activity 1.6 – Today Vs. Someday

Overview: Students will identify skills and interests and how they can influence future career choices and create a class book to display in the classroom.

ASCA National Competencies Addressed:
- Develop an awareness of personal abilities, skills, interests and motivations
- Pursue and develop competency in areas of interest

Materials: Book *Someday* by Eileen Spinelli, pencils, crayons/markers, worksheet "Today I... and Someday I might...."

Procedures:

1. Tell students that today we are going to focus on what you might want to be when you grow up. On the count of three, whisper out loud 2 careers you might want to have when you grow up.

2. Now, discuss how many of the skills practiced in school will help make a strong connection to the future.

3. Extend this conversation to how the career you whispered has to do with something you are good at now.

4. Let's read a book about a little girl who thinks about things she is good at today and how someday those things might lead to a career.

5. Read *Someday* by Spinelli.

6. After reading the story, create a T chart where students brainstorm a skill/interest they have today and then the career it might lead to in the future.

7. After a few examples, show the students the worksheet on page 25 and create some example pages.

8. Distribute Worksheet 1.6A and encourage students to create a good drawing because their "boss" (aka teacher) will be looking at it. (These pages can be complied into a class book with attached cover page to be displayed during conference week, etc. so their "boss" from home might see it too).

Activity 1.6a

Someday I might be...

Today I ....

Never stop dreaming. Yesterday's dream can become the reality of tomorrow.

Activity 1.6b - Class Book Cover Page

A book written by our class with our counselor about what we are good at today and how that will help us in the future.

Today We Are in _____'s Class But Someday...

26 • ©YouthLight

Activity 1.7 – Compare and Contrast

You may be interested in more than one career and that's normal. Some careers have a lot in common and some are very different. We learn more about ourselves – our likes and dislikes – when we compare careers that interest us.

Directions: Place the titles of two careers in the blanks. Within each circle, write words or short phrases that describe that career. Descriptions that are the same for both careers should be placed in the center circle.

CAREER 1 _____   **CAREER 2** _____

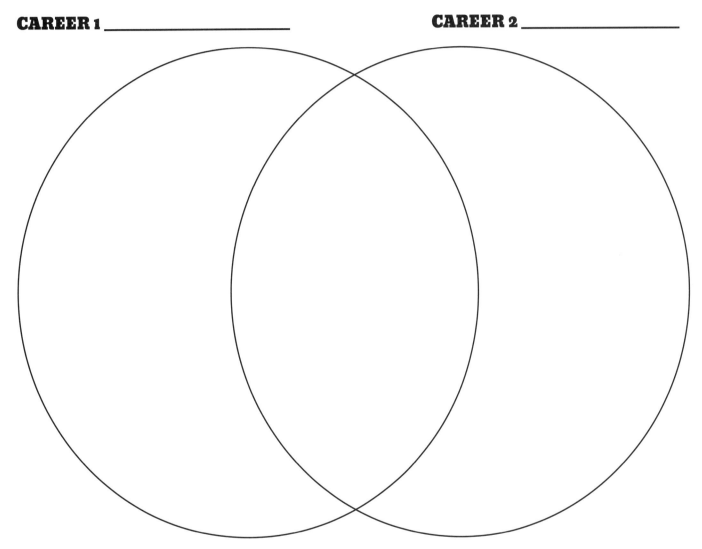

Consider these things:
- Works mostly inside or outside?
- Works mostly with people or things?
- Travels a lot for the job or works mostly in one place.
- Is a dangerous job or not?
- Needs lots of school/college training or on-the-job training?
- Need to wear a uniform or can wear any kinds of clothes.
- Works mostly at night or mostly in the day?
- Is a job where you get dirty or stay clean?

Activity 1.8 – Roll a Career Question

Use a pair of dice (one with numbers and one blank die that you can put dots of color). Have students work in groups to roll the dice to determine which questions to answer

ROLL A QUESTION: CAREER

	1	2	3	4	5	6
RED	Do 5 Jumping Jacks.	Think about a cool job you have heard about and describe that job.	What does work ethic mean?	If a police officer didn't try their best, what do you think might happen?	What jobs do people in your family have?	What subject would you need to be good at in order to be a doctor?
BLUE	What is something that you like doing after school?	What famous person do you think works hard at their job and why?	Name someone in your class who always works really hard.	Name 2 words that your teacher would use to describe you.	Go up to a teacher in the room and say, "Thanks for all you do."	Who is a grown up that you admire and why?
GREEN	Would you ever want a career where you could be famous? Why or why not?	Name something that is hard for you and how you work at getting better at it.	Give yourself a pat on the back and a big hug…just because!	Do you want to go to college when you grow up.	If a student is very creative, what are 2 careers they might want when they get older?	Why is getting along with others important in any career?
ORANGE	Give someone in the group a high 5.	Name 2 jobs you would never want.	Would you rather have a night time job or day time job?	Ask another player to tell about what a grown up in their family does for a job.	Ask your group to say this out loud, "We are professional students."	What would happen if a grown up was disrespectful to their boss at work?
PURPLE	Who is the hardest working person in your family?	What would happen if teachers decided not to work very hard?	What would be a reward you would want from your boss?	Name someone in your class who would be a good teacher when they grow up.	What are 2 careers you think you would be good at.	When you get older, what are 2 careers that you might want.
BLACK	Would you want a job working with animals? Why or why not?	What are 2 reasons that people have jobs.	What are 2 things that you are responsible for at school?	Say out loud, "I am pretty awesome!"	Why is it important for doctors to try their best?	Would you want to have an inside job or outside job?

Activity 1.9 – Snowmen at Work

Overview: Students will understand their interests and how that might affect their career choices.

ASCA National Competencies Addressed:
- Learn about the variety of traditional and nontraditional occupations.
- Develop an awareness of personal abilities, skills, interests and motivations.
- Learn how to interact cooperatively in teams.

Materials/Resources: *Snowmen at Work* by Carolyn Buehner, attached documents, construction paper, glue sticks, scissors

Procedures:
1. Define "career" and ask students what their parents do for careers. Ask students to say out loud a career that they would like to do when they grow up.
2. Read *Snowmen at Work*, pointing out while reading the differences in jobs the snowmen have. Do they work indoors or outdoors, with people or things, if they use their hands, if they help people, if they drive around or go to one place.
3. Tell students they are now going to have a chance to think about some of their interests and how that might influence what they want to have in a job.
4. Show students an example of a snowman that you built.
5. Distribute the snowman circles and have students cut these out and glue onto construction paper.
6. Distribute the Snowman Career Key/cutouts to the students. Discuss with students each choice along the way: "If you would like to work indoors like the dentist or the librarian in the book, choose a leaf for your snowman's head. If you would like to work outdoors like the fireman or pizza deliverer, put a snowflake on your snowman's head." With each decoration choice, relate back to a snowman's career in the book.
7. To conclude, have a student come up to show his/her snowman and see if the class can look at the key poster and explain their career interests. Students can look at the shapes and guess their classmates' career interests. For example, "You like to work indoors, with people, going to one place each day, and to help people."
8. Have students share their snowmen with a partner. For students who are up for the challenge, have them decide if these interests coincide with the career that they mentioned earlier.

Worksheet 1.9a

Snowman Career Key

Head Decoration
Indoors: Leaf
Outdoors: Snowflake

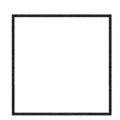

Eyes
Work with food: Squares
Work with people: Snowflake

Worksheet 1.9a

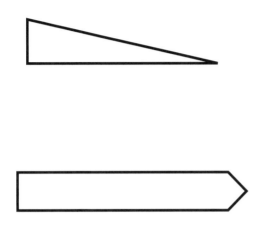

Nose
Travel or Drive: Triangle
Go to a place: Pentagon

Buttons
Help people: Hearts
Work with your hands: Circles

Worksheet 1.9b

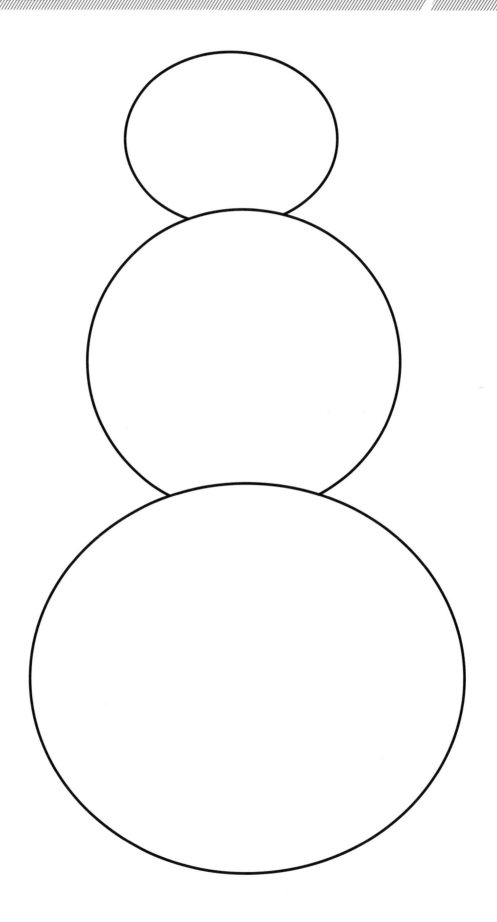

32 • ©YouthLight

Activity 1.10 – How On Earth Do You Get a Job?

Overview: This is a lesson where some vocabulary is pre-taught to give a better understanding of the book that will be read. Skills will be reviewed such as writing resumés and answering interview questions.

ASCA National Competencies Addressed:
- Develop an awareness of personal abilities, skills, interests and motivations
- Demonstrate knowledge of the career-planning process

Materials: *How to Get a Job by Me the Boss* by Sally Lloyd-Jones, worksheet number

Procedures:

1. Tell students that we will review terms that will be in the book we will read. (You can pre-teach/review these terms by having them on a chart, a powerpoint, or the board. Alternatively, you can have the students complete the crossword on page 20 that reviews many of the terms in the book.)

   Terms to review are:
   - **Career:** work, job or occupation.
   - **Employed:** someone who is working and getting paid for it.
   - **Resumé:** a piece of paper that states your work experience and qualifications that is given to someone who you want to hire you.
   - **Job Application:** a written form filled out in order to be considered for a job.
   - **References:** a person who can provide a letter or phone call to talk about your ability or reliability, used when applying for a new job.
   - **Interview:** a formal meeting where someone answers questions as they are trying to get hired for a job.

2. After reading the story, *How to get a Job by Me the Boss* by Sally Lloyd-Jones, distribute worksheet 1.10b on page 35 to the class. Instruct students to fill out the job application for a job that they might one day want (anything from working at a fast food restaurant, babysitting, teacher, lawyer, etc.)

3. Allow students to fill out applications. Simultaneously, while students are filling out applications, invite students who would like to sign up to do a mock interview. Call these students over to a small table and ask them the interview questions on page 34. (Option: Copy activity 1.10a on page 34 on the back of the job application, so students can look over questions prior to the mock interview).

Optional: Allow students to create their own resumé using the following link:

https://www.careerkids.com/resumeSSL.php

Activity 1.10a – Important Things to Know about Job Interviews

What is an interview? An interview is a formal meeting where someone answers questions as they are trying to get hired for a job. Interview skills must be learned. Think about these skills as you have your pretend interview:

- **Eye contact:** Look at the person who is asking you questions in the eyes.

- **Memory:** Remember the interviewers name and even say it out loud when you meet him/her, "Nice to meet you, Ms. King."

- **Articulation:** Speak slowly, clearly and with correct grammar.

- **Appropriate dress:** Wear professional looking clothing.

- **Answer Questions:** Make sure you are completely answering the questions.

- **Thoughtful questions:** Come into interviews with questions you might have about the job you are interviewing for.

Pretend/Mock Interview Questions:

- Why would you be good for this job?
- Tell about your experiences that will help you be good at this job.
- What is one of the best things about you?
- What would your past bosses (or teachers) say about you?
- How do you get along with others?

After your teacher or counselor does a mock/pretend interview, they might tell you who is most likely to get the job they interviewed for.

Activity 1.10b – Worksheet

JOB APPLICATION

Directions: Print clearly in black or blue ink. Answer all questions. Sign and date the form.

> **POSITION/JOB YOU ARE APPLYING FOR:** _____

> **PERSONAL INFORMATION:**

Name _____

Street Address _____

City, State, Zip Code _____

Phone Number (_____)_____

Days/Hours Available _____

> **EDUCATION:**

Name of School and Last Grade Completed:
_____

Honors/Awards: _____

Experiences, skills and qualifications that would help with this job:
_____
_____

> **REFERENCES:**

Name/How do you know them? _____
_____

Name/How do you know them? _____
_____

I promise that the information above is either true or pretend. I understand that if this was a real application, false information may be grounds for not hiring me or for immediate termination of employment at any point in the future if I am hired.

Applicant Signature_____ Date_____

©YouthLight • 35

Activity 1.11 – Career Awareness Secret Message

Overview: Students will complete these math problems to reveal a secret code. The code will reveal a sentence that will lead to a discussion about skills, interests, and making money as showed in the Venn Diagram on page 37.

ASCA National Competencies Addressed:
- Develop an awareness of personal abilities, skills, interests and motivations
- Pursue and develop competency in areas of interest

Materials: Career Awareness Secret Code Worksheet, Career Awareness Venn Poster

Procedures:

1. Have students complete Career Awareness Secret Message.
2. In dyads, have students discuss what this means. (Answer: Skills + Interests + Makes $ = Great Career Choice).
3. Label Venn with these 3 items in the outer circle. Where the three overlap, write "Dream Job."
4. Show poster on page 38. Discuss how these diagrams are the same. (ie: Skill = What you are good at. Interest = what you like)

Activity 1.11a – Career Awareness Secret Message I

Directions: In the key, each letter has a number under it. In the puzzle, you will figure out the secret message by writing the letter above each number that you find in the key. For example, in key 13 is written under the letter S. So the letter of the first word in the is S.

Break the code and find out a message about how to find a career that will be right for you.

Key:

A	B	C	D	E	F	G	H	I	J	K	L	M	N	O	P	Q	R	S	T	U	V	W	X	Y	Z
3	6	19		4	14	11	1	2		26	5						8	13	17			0	9		7

Puzzle:

S __ __ __ __ __
13 16 2 5 3 13   +

__ __ __ __ __ __ __ __ __
2 18 17 4 8 12 13 17 13   +

__ __ __ __ __ = __ __ __ __ __ __ __ __ __ __
20 3 26 4 $ 11 6+2 4 4 17 19 1 8 4 4 8

__ __ __ __ __ __
19 1 22 2 19 4

{ Your counselor will tell you how to fill in this Venn Diagram. }

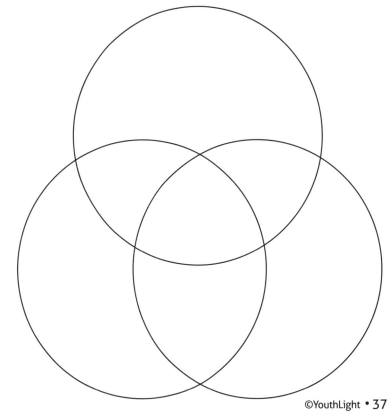

Activity 1.11b – Career Awareness Secret Message II

Directions: In the Key, each letter has a number under it. In the puzzle, you will figure out the secret message by writing the letter above each number that the math problem represents. For example in first problem 10+3= 13, and in the key 13 is written under the letter S. So the letter of the first letter of the first word is an S.

Break the code and find out a message about how to find a career that will be right for you.

Key:

A	B	C	D	E	F	G	H	I	J	K	L	M	N	O	P	Q	R	S	T	U	V	W	X	Y	Z
3	6	19		4	14	11	1	2		26	5						8	13	17			0	9		7

Puzzle:

S ___ ___ ___ ___ ___
10+3 10+16 1+1 2+3 4-1 8+5   +

___ ___ ___ ___ ___ ___ ___ ___ ___
2-0 11+7 9+8 1+3 12-4 16-4 11+2 9+8 26-13   +

___ ___ ___ ___ ___   ___ ___ ___ ___ ___ ___ ___ ___ ___ ___ ___
10+10 6-3 19+7 5-1 $ = 22-11 6+2 13-9 7-4 12+5 10+9 4-3 4+4 10-6 2+2 7+1

___ ___ ___ ___ ___ ___
12+7 9-8 11+12 7-5 6+13 9-5

{ Your counselor will tell you how to fill in this Venn Diagram. }

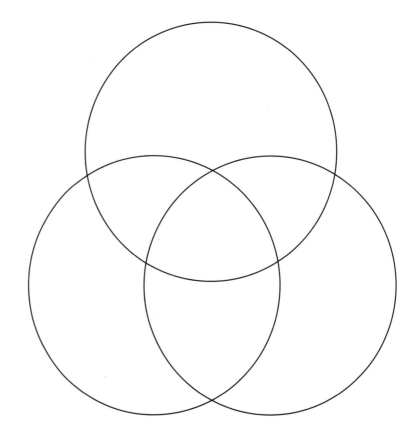

38 • ©YouthLight

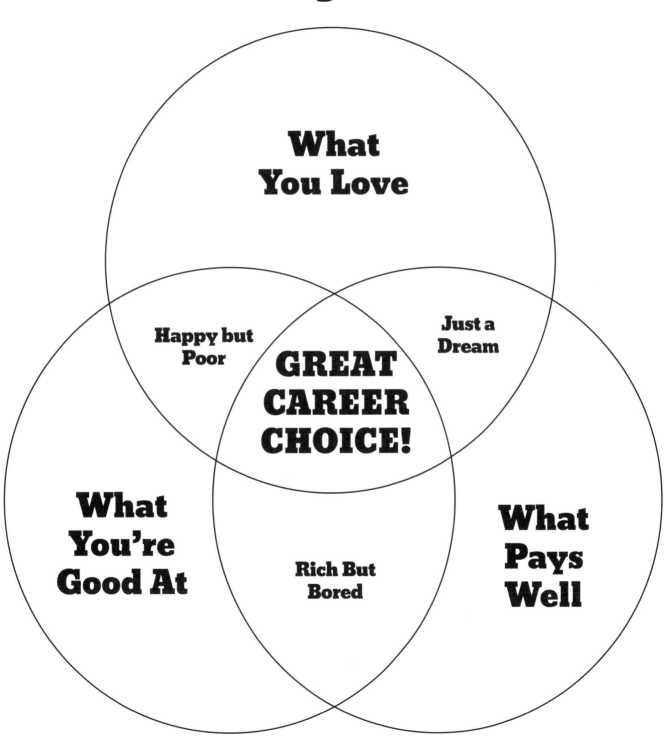

Activity 1.12 – Career Ice Cream Sundae

Overview: This would be a great activity to do as a culmination of career awareness. The reproducible activity reviews tools needed on jobs, character traits and education needed.

ASCA National Competencies Addressed:
• Pursue and develop competency in areas of interest

Materials: Worksheet 1.12a on page 41, construction paper, glue, scissors

Procedures:

1. Discuss with students the importance of exploring paths to future careers.

2. Tell students that we will create a delicious art project to display their knowledge about career awareness.

3. Distribute the following worksheet (page 41) and a piece of construction paper. Students will need scissors and crayons, markers or colored pencils and glue stick.

4. Students will use the key on the worksheet to label each item.
- Dish: Name of Job
- Whipped Cream: Education/Training Needed
- Ice Cream Scoops: 2 responsibilities of the job
- Spoon: Character traits needed to do the job well
- Strawberries: 3 tools needed for this job

Worksheet 1.12a

Whipped Cream: Education/Training Needed

Ice Cream Scoops: 2 Responsibilities of the job

Strawberries: 3 tools needed for this job

Spoon: What character traits are needed to do the job well

Dish: Name of Job

Cookie: Career Cluster

Activity 1.13 – Career Wax Museum

Overview: Students will choose a career that they would like to present and then the class will establish a career

ASCA National Competencies Addressed:
- Learn about the variety of traditional and nontraditional occupations.

Materials: Worksheet 1.13a, materials needed to present different careers at the wax museum (counselor can gather or students can be assigned to bring these from home.)

Procedures:

1. Tell students that they are going to choose a career to find some facts about. They are then going to gather information about it into a short speech, which they will say when they dress up as that career person at the school's Career Wax Museum.

2. Distribute Worksheet 1.13a to guide students into forming ideas for what career wax figure/person they want to represent.

3. Send home the Career Wax Museum Checklist (page 44) with students so that they can be prepared for the event. (Feel free to write the date of the event on the checklist if you want to invite parents. It's always good PR!)

4. Students can create a button or another symbol that will cause them to speak.

5. At the Career Wax Museum, each student will be dressed up as their person and be "frozen" as a wax figure until someone comes up to them. At that point the student will "come to life" and say their short speech, explaining about that career.

Activity 1.13a – Career Wax Museum

Directions: Imagine you are a wax figure in a "Career Wax Museum." Others will come to this museum and press a button to "activate" wax figures to hear what their career is all about. What career would you want to represent in a wax museum?

My Job

What career "wax figure" would you like to be? _____

Below, answer questions to give you an idea of what you (as a career wax figure) would say when someone comes by and wants to hear about you. Use your imagination about what this career person does.

❯ What you do during your hours each day at your job/career? _____
_____

❯ What do you need to wear at your job and why? _____
_____

❯ What tools do you use and why? _____
_____

This job is important because:
_____
_____
_____
_____

This is your wax museum button. Write the career you will represent and decorate it. ➡

Press here to learn about my career. I am a...

©YouthLight • 43

Activity 1.13b – Career Wax Museum Checklist

Career Wax Museum Checklist

Name _____

Parents/Guardians,

Below is a checklist to help your child get ready for the Career Wax Museum that we are preparing. Thank you for helping him/her with this checklist so that he/she will be ready.

- ____ Prepare: Fill out the "My Job" sheet. (done in school)
- ____ Write: Create a one paragraph description of your job.
- ____ Collect: Collect clothes for your costume.
- ____ Select: Select props that go with your job.
- ____ Practice: Practice reading your paragraph aloud slowly and clearly. (Practicing for friends or family is a great idea. It will also help you to practice doing it in the mirror... even if it feels silly!)

Career Wax Museum Checklist

Name _____

Parents/Guardians,

Below is a checklist to help your child get ready for the Career Wax Museum that we are preparing. Thank you for helping him/her with this checklist so that he/she will be ready.

- ____ Prepare: Fill out the "My Job" sheet. (done in school)
- ____ Write: Create a one paragraph description of your job.
- ____ Collect: Collect clothes for your costume.
- ____ Select: Select props that go with your job.
- ____ Practice: Practice reading your paragraph aloud slowly and clearly. (Practicing for friends or family is a great idea. It will also help you to practice doing it in the mirror... even if it feels silly!)

Activity 1.14 – Career Family/Community Tree

Overview: Students will explore careers in their families and decide which interests them most.

ASCA National Competencies Addressed:
- Learn about the variety of traditional and nontraditional occupations.

Materials: *The Night Worker* by Kate Banks, Worksheet 1.14A

Procedures:

1. Ask students to close their eyes and think about what family members do for work. Ask, "Do you know what your mom, dad, aunt, uncle, grandparents, cousins do/did for work? What about family friends or people you admire?

2. Share about what your family members do/did for careers. Also share what the people you admire do for work (this is especially for the kids who do not live with immediate family or do not aspire to go down the same path as their family members).

3. Read *The Night Worker* by Kate Banks

4. Discuss how some children want to work in similar jobs as someone in their family, but sometimes they don't. Who wants to tell why they would or would not want to work in the same field as a grown-up they know? For example, my father is a doctor. I would not like that job because I think blood is yucky. My aunt was a teacher, and I like kids, so that is something I might want to do.

5. Distribute worksheet 1.14A and guide students to think about what the following people do for a job and label the worksheet accordingly (Dad: Doctor, Aunt: Teacher, Ms. King: school counselor, Mr. Potts: bus driver, Julie my cousin: Chef)

"Career Family/Community Tree" note to parents below:

Dear parent/guardian:

Your child is working on a Career Family/Community Tree project for class. It would be helpful if you can fill out this list with your child about their family or close family friends, hopefully spanning generations. This will help them understand their family history and make connections with people in their lives as they plan for their own futures. We will create a product using this information. I appreciate your assistance with this assignment.

Sincerely,

Here is a list of people in _____'s life and some of the careers/jobs they have had.

Name	Relationship to student	Careers
1. _____	_____	_____
2. _____	_____	_____
3. _____	_____	_____
4. _____	_____	_____
5. _____	_____	_____

Activity 1.14a – Worksheet

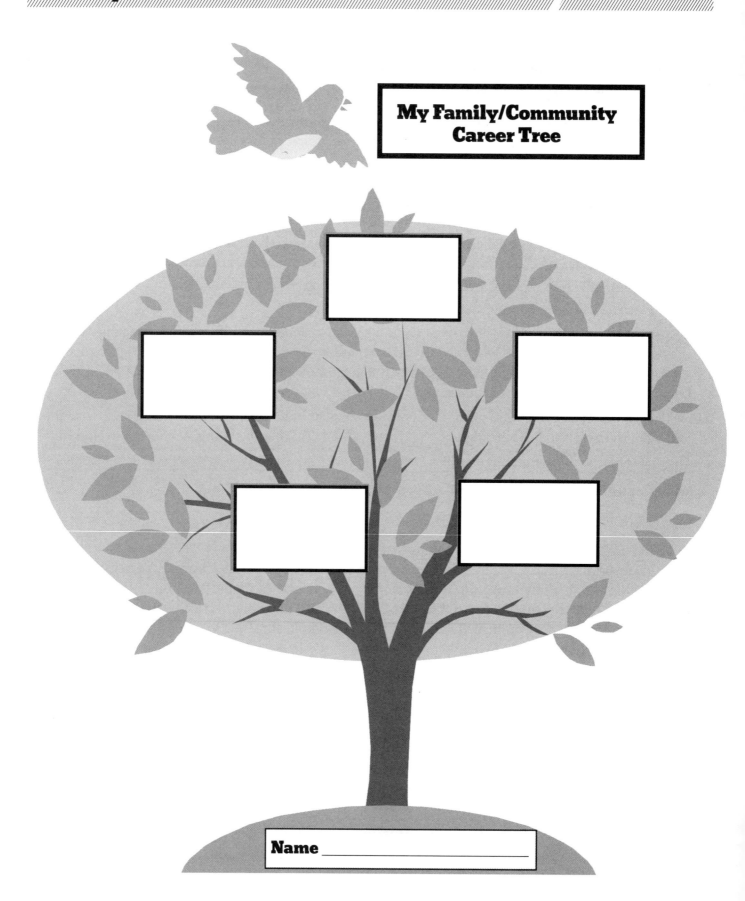

Activity 1.15 – Career Connections with School Subjects

Name _____

Directions: Look at the career in the left column then, go across the row and check each box if you think you will need to be good in that subject for that particular job.

	Math	Reading	Writing	Science	Social Studies	Art	Music	PE
Doctor								
Farmer								
Cashier								
Chef								
Video Game Designer								
Banker								
NFL Football Player								

©YouthLight • 47

Activity 1.16 – Career Inventory

Name _____

Directions Part 1: Circle any of the statements in the boxes below that describe you.

PEOPLE	DATA/INFORMATION	THINGS
I like to help friends with their problems.	I like science experiments.	I am good at building things.
I like to do group activities.	I am good at staying on a schedule.	I enjoy making crafts.
I am cheerful toward others.	I pay close attention to details.	I prefer to work alone.
I am a leader.	I like to stay organized.	I ask questions about how machines work.
I am good at teaching others.	I figure out math problems for fun.	If something is broken, I can usually fix it.
△	△	△

Directions Part 2: Now that you are done, go back and count the circles in each column and put that number in the triangle in the bottom row of the column. In which column do you have the biggest number: People, Data, or Things? This means that when you get older you might like to work in a career where you work with _____.

48 • ©YouthLight

Activity 1.17 – Cocoa Bean to Chocolate Showdown

Overview: In this game, teams brainstorm how many people it takes to make and distribute different objects. This lesson will inspire discussion about how many different careers are involved with one product."

ASCA National Competencies Addressed:
- Learn to work cooperatively with others as a team member
- Identify Attitudes and behaviors which lead to successful learning

Materials: Needed Copies of worksheet for each team.

Procedures:

1. Read from *Cocoa Bean to Chocolate Showdown* and discuss the different jobs that were involved.

2. Divide students into groups of 4 or 5 students per team (or have them divide themselves into groups). Have students who are struggling to find a group come stand with you and you can find them a team.

3. Distribute a copy of worksheet to each team.

4. Explain the rules to the game. "I will give each team 1 minute to come up with as many answers as possible to the question I ask. Once the time is up, I will say pencils down. I will ask one team to read their answers one by one and if anyone else has that answer everyone with that answer has to cross that off. Your team will get points for any answer that is not crossed off."

5. Let's look at the sample. If the question is, List as many careers as possible that have to do with chocolate, you and your team will need to brainstorm. (see example).

6. Next round:
- Video Games
- Bread
- Pencils
- Apple Juice

7. Extend this lesson by having students match the jobs they came up with to the appropriate career cluster.

Worksheet 1.17a – Cocoa Bean to Chocolate Showdown

No matter what you choose for your career, you will always have to get along with the people around you. Look at the sample and listen to the directions for this game.

Points:_____

Example: List as many careers as possible that have to do with _____ chocolate_____.

1. ~~Farmer picks the cocoa beans.~~
2. Chocolate factory worker.
3. Grocer who sells it.
4. Truck driver who delivers it.
5. Chef who created it.
6. Sales person who sells it to grocer.

Round 1: List as many careers as possible that have to do with _____.

Round 2: List as many careers as possible that have to do with _____.

Round 3: List as many careers as possible that have to do with _____.

Activity 1.18 – Career Day Reflections

"The Most Important Job is that of a Student!"
(But for now, I need to learn about careers in the community.)

My Career Stations:

1. _____ 2. _____

3. _____ 4. _____

#1 Career: _____

What Career Cluster is this job?
- ☐ Science, Technology, Engineering,
- ☐ Math (STEM)
- ☐ Business Management or
- ☐ Administration
- ☐ Manufacturing
- ☐ Architecture and Construction
- ☐ Health Sciences
- ☐ Agriculture
- ☐ Transportation, Logistics
- ☐ Energy
- ☐ Hospitality
- ☐ Finance
- ☐ Education and Training
- ☐ Government
- ☐ Arts, AV and Communication
- ☐ Architecture and Construction
- ☐ Information Technology
- ☐ Law and Public Safety
- ☐ Human Services
- ☐ Marketing and Advertising

Something you learned/found surprising:

_____
_____
_____
_____
_____
_____
_____
_____

Does this job require special training?	YES	NO
Does this job require a college education?	YES	NO
Is this a job you are interested in?	YES	NO

#2 Career: _____

What Career Cluster is this job?
- ☐ Science, Technology, Engineering,
- ☐ Math (STEM)
- ☐ Business Management or
- ☐ Administration
- ☐ Manufacturing
- ☐ Architecture and Construction
- ☐ Health Sciences
- ☐ Agriculture
- ☐ Transportation, Logistics
- ☐ Energy
- ☐ Hospitality
- ☐ Finance
- ☐ Education and Training
- ☐ Government
- ☐ Arts, AV and Communication
- ☐ Architecture and Construction
- ☐ Information Technology
- ☐ Law and Public Safety
- ☐ Human Services
- ☐ Marketing and Advertising

Something you learned/found surprising:

_____
_____
_____
_____
_____
_____
_____
_____

Does this job require special training?	YES	NO
Does this job require a college education?	YES	NO
Is this a job you are interested in?	YES	NO

Activity 1.18 – Career Day Reflections

#3 Career: _____

What Career Cluster is this job?
- ☐ Science, Technology, Engineering,
- ☐ Math (STEM)
- ☐ Business Management or
- ☐ Administration
- ☐ Manufacturing
- ☐ Architecture and Construction
- ☐ Health Sciences
- ☐ Agriculture
- ☐ Transportation, Logistics
- ☐ Energy
- ☐ Hospitality
- ☐ Finance
- ☐ Education and Training
- ☐ Government
- ☐ Arts, AV and Communication
- ☐ Architecture and Construction
- ☐ Information Technology
- ☐ Law and Public Safety
- ☐ Human Services
- ☐ Marketing and Advertising

Something you learned/found surprising:

_____
_____
_____
_____
_____
_____
_____
_____

Does this job require special training?	YES	NO
Does this job require a college education?	YES	NO
Is this a job you are interested in?	YES	NO

#4 Career: _____

What Career Cluster is this job?
- ☐ Science, Technology, Engineering,
- ☐ Math (STEM)
- ☐ Business Management or
- ☐ Administration
- ☐ Manufacturing
- ☐ Architecture and Construction
- ☐ Health Sciences
- ☐ Agriculture
- ☐ Transportation, Logistics
- ☐ Energy
- ☐ Hospitality
- ☐ Finance
- ☐ Education and Training
- ☐ Government
- ☐ Arts, AV and Communication
- ☐ Architecture and Construction
- ☐ Information Technology
- ☐ Law and Public Safety
- ☐ Human Services
- ☐ Marketing and Advertising

Something you learned/found surprising:

_____
_____
_____
_____
_____
_____
_____
_____

Does this job require special training?	YES	NO
Does this job require a college education?	YES	NO
Is this a job you are interested in?	YES	NO

What was something all of these jobs had in common? _____
_____

Is training important in a career? _____
_____

What is one thing that you think was important from today's presentations. _____
_____

Worksheet 1.19 – Create a Database of Career Speakers

Set this sign-up sheet out for parents at Open House. They can sign up to come talk to classes about their careers.

Parents: It is nver too early to help students understand how the lessons we teach can translate into real world experience. If you are willing to help out our school by talking about your career at some point in the year, please sign below. Check off what category/cluster your job falls under. We appreciate your partnership in helping our students understand the connection between school and the world of work.

Teacher Name: _____

Sign Up Today!

Parent Name:	Agriculture	Arts, AV, and Construction	Business Admin	Education and Training	Energy	Finance	Government and Public Admin.	Health Science	Hospitality and Tourism	Human Services	Information Technology	Law and Public Safety	Manufacturing	Marketing	STEM (Science, Technology, Engineering & Math)	Transportation, Distribution & Logistics

Also, please sign here if you have a job with a career vehicle that we could invite to Careers on Wheels: _____

Activity 1.20 – Career Centers

Preparation:

A center-based lesson can be done in a separate counselor's room if it is large enough, or if there is an empty classroom you can borrow, or centers can be brought into a classroom as mobile centers. Typically, there are 4 centers and 5-7 kids in each group that rotate to each center. Each center lasts about 6 minutes. The counselor rings the bell so that the students know it is time to rotate to the next center.

Sample 30 minute lesson:

Introduction/Explanation of Centers to Whole Class: 4 minutes

Split Students into groups: 1 minute

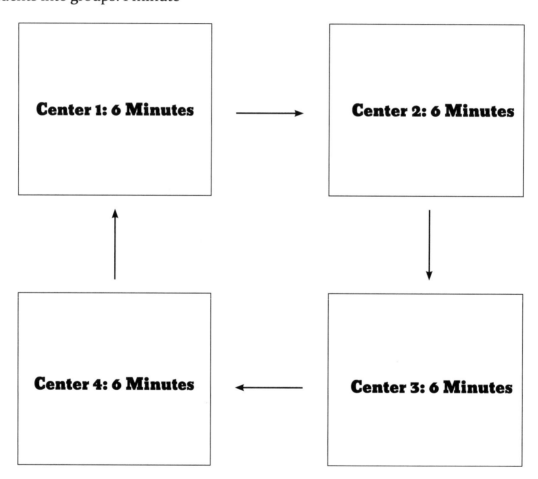

Choose 4 of the following activities (one for each center):

– Career Inventory (page 48)

– Puzzle Center: Offer the Maze (page 18), Word Search (see page 19), or Crossword (page 20)

– Find a suitable video Clip on YouTube, etc. (must be 4-6 minutes in length for it to work appropriately)

– Silent Reading Center (Choose appropriate books from pages 15-16 to have students read silently)

– Career Magic Square

Chapter 2: Work Ethic

The elevator to success is not running; you must climb the stairs – Zig Ziglar

ASCA Competencies addressed in this chapter:
• Student will learn to demonstrate dependability, productivity and initiative.

• Display a positive interest in learning

• Take pride in work and achievement

Chapter Introduction
Students need to understand why work ethic can be even more important than how "smart" they are. In this chapter, students can explore why doing your best is a skill that needs to be mastered early on.

Activity	Page #	Chapter Contents
2.0	56	Literature Link
2.1	58	Counselor Connection Card
2.2	59	Poem: What is Work Ethic
2.3	60	Cryptogram
2.4	61	Do Your Best Story / Make and Take Magnet
2.5	66	Making your Mark (create stamp from bottle cap)
2.6	67	Roll a Question
2.7	68	Color in Poster
2.8	69	Good to Great
2.9	70	Step 1,2, 3 Goal: Build a Snowman
2.10	72	Famous Failures

The only place where success comes before work is in the dictionary.

- Donald Kendall

Activity 2.0 – Literature Link: Work Ethic

Below are books that will correlate with work ethic and doing your best. There is a line before each book so that you can mark where it is located, so that if you decide to use it in a lesson you know where to find it. (Personal Library, Media Center, online audiobook, Public Library, or Need to Order it)

_____ ***Back to Front and Upside Down* by Claire Alexander** – Stan wants to make a birthday card for Mr. Slippers, the principal. But when he tries to write, his words come out all wrong. He is afraid to ask for help because he thinks everyone will laugh at him. Students will empathize with Stan's fears and learn the importance of asking for help.

_____ ***The Dot* by Peter Reynolds** – This is a story about how confidence comes along with competence. Wise advice, offered by her teacher, sets our main character on a journey of success. Vashti at first seems beaten by the blank paper before her, but in the end becomes the most competent type of learner ... a teacher.

_____ ***Tops and Bottoms* by Janet Stevens** – In this story of hard work paying off, Hare decides it's time to buy his own land back from his neighbor Bear, who sleeps through his work days. He makes a deal with his neighbor and the two become business partners. In the end, Bear learns the benefits of hard work and Hare earns enough money to buy back his own land again.

_____ ***The Boy Who Harnessed the Wind* by William Kamkwamba and Bryan Mealer** – This is a story of a boy growing up in Malawi where he was forced to drop out of school. While educating himself in a library, he sees a textbook from the United States that shows a windmill, and decides to build one to power his home. Set in a background of poverty, this is the journey of a boy who believes in himself and becomes a young scientist.

_____ ***Last to Finish: A Story About the Smartest Boy in Math Class (The Adventures of Everyday Geniuses)* by Barbara Esham** – This is a great book for any student who is anxious about learning or taking tests. Any student who has gotten butterflies in their stomach over a test or felt the frustration of being the last one to finish, will identify with this story.

_____ ***Can I Have Some Money?: Max Gets It!* By Candi Sparks** – This book helps students make the connection between earning money and having the ability to buy things you want. The book expands on the basic concept of money by introducing the importance of saving, credit and budgeting.

_____ ***Princesses are Not Quitters* by Kate Lum** – Three Princesses jealously watch three servant girls "out doing interesting things" and decide to swap jobs for a day. Once the royal divas realize how hard the chores are, they look forward to their life as princesses again, but they now have an appreciation for hard work.

_____ ***Wilma Unlimited* by Kathleen Krull** – This story of Wilma Rudolph's incredible courage and perseverance takes us on her life journey overcoming a disability to ultimately win gold medals in the Olympics.

_____ ***Winners Never Quit* by Mia Hamm** – Little Mia's favorite part of soccer is to win and score goals. She has to learn to be happy to just have fun, and she learns that trying your best is all that truly matters.

_____ ***Edgar the Eagle in Do Your Best!* By Sheila Hairston** – Edgar is excited about the eagle flying show. He practices until one day he breaks his wing! How will he ever be able to compete? A great story for teaching people about not giving up, trying your hardest, and that winning is not the most important.

_____ ***I Will Try* by Marilyn Janovitz** – Ella wishes she could be like Jan, the best one in her gymnastics class. Jan can spin and leap on the balance beam. Can Ella? Her first attempt is a failure, and Ella is ready to quit. But Jan is great at being a friend too and with her support, Ella tries again and succeeds.

_____ ***Long Shot: Never Too Small to Dream Big Hardcover* by Chris Paul** – Even though he was small, Chris loved to play basketball. He ignored all the people that told him that he couldn't succeed, because he had big dreams.

_____ ***Pepper Parrot's Problem with Patience: A Captain No Beard Story* by Carole P. Roman** – On a ship, the crew learns that new crewmate Pepper Parrot is having trouble with certain drills. Pepper doesn't know her right from her left side, so problems arise over and over. They teach her a trick to learn the difference between her right and left and there is a great lesson on dealing with frustrations. The book reviews that there are always others around who are willing to help.

Activity 2.1 – Work Ethic: Counselor Connection Card

Directions: After a lesson on Work Ethic and Motivation is taught, give students a counselor connection card. If they bring it back by a designated date, they are eligible to win a prize. You can draw several cards that have been signed and returned and give those students a prize.

Counselor Connection Card: Work Ethic

This week in our lesson, we reviewed the importance of working hard. Kids learn best by watching the adults around them. Talk to your child about what keeps you motivated to do your best. In your discussion, give an example about something that was difficult for you when you were in school and how you worked hard to achieve success. Also, you can ask your child what helps keep them motivated. You might be surprised at the answers!

Signing this Counselor Connection Card means you have discussed with your child why having a strong work ethic is important.

Student Name _____
Homeroom _____
Adult Signature _____

Counselor Connection Card: Work Ethic

This week in our lesson, we reviewed the importance of working hard. Kids learn best by watching the adults around them. Talk to your child about what keeps you motivated to do your best. In your discussion, give an example about something that was difficult for you when you were in school and how you worked hard to achieve success. Also, you can ask your child what helps keep them motivated. You might be surprised at the answers!

Signing this Counselor Connection Card means you have discussed with your child why having a strong work ethic is important.

Student Name _____
Homeroom _____
Adult Signature _____

Counselor Connection Card: Work Ethic

This week in our lesson, we reviewed the importance of working hard. Kids learn best by watching the adults around them. Talk to your child about what keeps you motivated to do your best. In your discussion, give an example about something that was difficult for you when you were in school and how you worked hard to achieve success. Also, you can ask your child what helps keep them motivated. You might be surprised at the answers!

Signing this Counselor Connection Card means you have discussed with your child why having a strong work ethic is important.

Student Name _____
Homeroom _____
Adult Signature _____

Counselor Connection Card: Work Ethic

This week in our lesson, we reviewed the importance of working hard. Kids learn best by watching the adults around them. Talk to your child about what keeps you motivated to do your best. In your discussion, give an example about something that was difficult for you when you were in school and how you worked hard to achieve success. Also, you can ask your child what helps keep them motivated. You might be surprised at the answers!

Signing this Counselor Connection Card means you have discussed with your child why having a strong work ethic is important.

Student Name _____
Homeroom _____
Adult Signature _____

Activity 2.2 – Poem

Directions: Think about a time when you didn't feel like doing something. As you read the poem, think about the "tug of war" that goes through your mind when struggle with wanting to complete a task. Draw a picture or comic of that time.

What is Work Ethic?

"I tried", Ann said at homework time, when really she was lazy
She thought excuses would be OK when her brain was tired and hazy.
Her mom knew "giving effort" is what it truly means to try
Not just staring at the page; giving up with a sigh
Cause some kids aren't good math at reading or at writing
But working hard no matter what, is worth internal fighting
The two small figures on your shoulders battle out their wills
"Yes, try hard" or "No, give up" a tug of war of skills
Who will win the war at last is really up to you
Finish strong or just give up …. It's time to think it through.

— By Lisa King

Activity 2.3 – Work Ethic Cryptogram

Directions: This puzzle is called a Cryptogram. At the top there is a KEY that lists all the letters from A thru Z with a box below. Each of the letters has a corresponding number; some are already shown. Fill in the letters that correspond to the numbers below the blanks to solve the phrase.

Key:

A	B	C	D	E	F	G	H	I	J	K	L	M	N	O	P	Q	R	S	T	U	V	W	X	Y	Z
			13	14							8			4			11	1				21			2

Puzzle:

```
T _ E     O _ L Y        _ L _ _ E     W _ E _ E
1 26 14   4 12 8 2       25 8 10 15 14  21 26 14 16 14

S _ _ _ E S S    _ O _ E S     _ E _ O _ E    W O _ _
11 19 15 15 14 11 11  15 4 23 14 11   3 14 17 4 16 14   21 4 16 18

_ S    _ _     T _ E     D _ _ T _ O _ _ _ Y .
5 11   5 12    1 26 14   13 5 15 1 5 4 12 10 16 2
```

Students, don't give up!!
Remember the point of this lesson is to learn about work ethic!

Activity 2.4 – Do Your Best Story

Overview: While this story could be read and used as a lesson unto itself, and so could the make and take project on page 64. These two parts put together create an informative and fun, creative lesson.

ASCA National Competencies Addressed:
- Students will learn to demonstrate dependability, productivity and initiative.
- Display a positive interest in learning
- Take pride in work and achievement

Materials: Foam shapes, magic markers, glue, magnetic discs or strong magnet tape, wooden clothespins, small labels or cuts outs that say "my best work."

Procedures:

1. Optional: Read story 2.4a on page 62 to lead into this activity.

2. After reading the story, tell class that we are going to make a "Best Work Magnet" just like they discussed in the story. (Show students an example of the magnet clip we will be making in class as an example of what Jada made in the story.)

3. Before starting the activity discuss these questions:
    - Why is it important to be proud of your work?
    - Do you like when your parents display your work at home?
    - What is the difference between bragging and being proud?
    - How can adults tell that you have tried your best on an assignment?
    - What are some benefits of doing your best work and not rushing through?

4. See activity instructions on page 64 and put these on a SmartBoard or for the students to see as they are creating their clips.

5. Distribute materials to each table of students so that each person has one of everything (wooden clothespin, foam shape, "my best work" cut out, glue, magnet).

6. Allow students to create their clothespin. (Note that you might need to have teachers clear a space so that these can dry).

Activity 2.4a – Best Work: Story Connection

Directions: After reading the story complete the worksheet that follows.

It was Friday after a rainy morning, and Jada looked at her paper and she knew it would take her forever. Mrs. Smith told the class that they could have free time once they each finished this assignment, but WOW... it was really long. So, Jada did what she always did; she rushed through her work. Messy handwriting, wrong answers, and she knew it. But, free time was what she had her eye on.

Logan and Jada got up at the same time to put their assignment in the "finished work" basket. When Mrs. Smith looked at Logan's paper, she smiled and said, "Thank you." When Jada turned in her paper, Mrs. Smith couldn't help but raise her eyebrows and make a face. "What?" asked Jada.

"Are you sure you want to turn this in?" her teacher asked.

"What do you mean?" Asked Jada, but she knew exactly what her teacher meant.

"Jada, you know that's not your best work," replied her teacher. I just know you can do better and I know you will feel better about it in the long run."

But the only thing Jada was thinking was, "Can I go have free time now?" Mrs. Smith pulled out a new blank worksheet, and pointed Jada towards her desk to start the assignment all over. By the time Jada was finished being mad, and completed her assignment again, playtime was over. Zero minutes of playtime!

The next Friday, when Mrs. Smith told the class that she would once again give them an assignment, and when they were finished they could have free time. Jada looked at the assignment. There were 10 questions that required answers in complete sentences. This would take forever!

Jada remembered the conversation she had with her Aunt Traci after last week's frustration. Aunt Traci had said to cover up all the questions except the one she was on. Aunt Traci said to take a deep breath if she got frustrated and also to check over her work once she was done.

Jada really wanted to just rush through, but last time rushing led to zero minutes of playtime. So, Jada tried to follow Aunt Traci's advice. When Jada was still working, other kids were getting finished, and this frustrated Jada, so she took a deep breath. When she thought she was done, she looked up at the clock, walked over to Mrs. Smith, and turned it in. She waited for the raised eyebrows, but instead Mrs. Smith turned to her with a huge smile. Jada looked behind her, thinking "Is she looking at me?"... but indeed she was.

After Jada enjoyed her sixteen minutes of free time, Mrs. Smith called the students to their desks. She told the class that today they would be doing an art project. She explained that they would be making "my best work magnets" so that each student could display their work at home in a special place. When Mrs. Smith showed the class a sample of what the magnet should look like, she put the magnet on the board with an example of someone's best work. Can you guess whose work was shown to the class?

Worksheet 2.4b

Name _____

Directions: After reading/hearing the story, complete the worksheet that follows.

What was Aunt Traci's advice to Jada? _____
_____
_____

What lesson do you think Jada learned? _____
_____
_____

Do you think that kids like to show off their great work to their parents? _____
_____
_____

Where would you want to hang your great work in your house for everyone to see? _____
_____

Activity 2.4c – Worksheet

Directions:

1. Peel sticker off back of magnet and place on the back of the clothes pin.

2. Decorate your "My Best Work" Shape. (on next page)

3. Glue the shape on the front side of the clothes pin.

4. Decorate!

Activity 2.4d – My Best Work Shapes

My Best Work

My Best Work

My Best Work

My Best Work

Activity 2.5 – Making Your Mark: What is Work Ethic?

Overview: This lesson will help students understand that their work habits will be evident to teachers, parents and other students. A good work ethic will help students know that working hard leads to success.

ASCA National Competencies Addressed:
- Student will learn to demonstrate dependability, productivity and initiative.
- Display a positive interest in learning
- Take pride in work and achievement

Materials: Step books (see pages 56-57) Book on work ethic (*Edgar the Eagle, Boy Who Harnessed the Wind, Wilma Unlimited*), inkpad

Procedures:
1. Ask students, "What is work ethic?" According to Dictionary.com the definition is: "Work ethic is a belief in importance of work."
2. Ask students, "How can we tell if a person has a good work ethic?" (Accept answers like: they will finish their work, go above and beyond, will end up with a better job, be smarter.)
3. Now think about what teachers think of you. When you turn in work do they think? Neat handwriting, perfectionist, rushes though, always tries hard?
4. Discuss the phrase "MAKING YOUR MARK" and how we each literally have a mark: a finger print!
5. Distribute (washable) ink pads to students. Choose from one of the following activities.
    - Allow students to make their own fingerprint stamp art.
    - This option requires preparation and could prove to be labor intensive. For this reason, this one might be best as a small group option or part 1 of a two-part lesson. Allow each student to make a clear thumbprint on a paper. Counselor can enlarge each it to a size where words can be written in between the lines. Encourage students to choose words that describe what type of student they are (responsible, thoughtful, quick, artistic, etc.). This can be titled: "this is how I make my mark: Work Ethic"
    - Make bottle top stamper by hot gluing a 1-2" foam shape to bottle tops that have been collected (If you ask your staff to put water bottle/soda plastic tops in a collection area, you will get a good collection quickly.)
6. For students who finish early, have Roll a Question (activity 2.6 available).

We found 89% of the time new hires failed, it was because of attitude.
– Mark Murphy

Share this quote with the students to reiterate what good work ethic means.

Activity 2.6 – Work Ethic: Roll a Question

Use a pair of dice (one with numbers and one blank die that you can put dots of color). Have students work in groups to roll the dice to determine which questions to answer.

	1	2	3	4	5	6
RED	Do you like to play first and then work or get work done before you play?	Think about an assignment that you have worked hard on and tell about it.	What does work ethic mean?	When you have a job and you choose not to do your best, what do you think might happen?	What would happen if teachers decided not to work very hard?	Do 5 Jumping Jacks.
BLUE	What is something that you are good at?	What famous person do you admire and why?	Name someone in your class who always works really hard.	Name 2 words that your teacher would use to describe you.	Go up to a teacher in the room and say, "Thanks for all you do."	Who is an adult that you want to be like when you grow up?
GREEN	What is a sport you are good at but want to get better?	Name something that is hard for you and how you work at getting better at it.	Give yourself a pat on the back and a big hug… just because!	Do you care if your friends see you get in trouble?	Why do teachers get frustrated when students don't check over their work?	Name one time that you learned from your mistakes.
ORANGE	Give someone in the group a high 5.	Name 2 things at home that keep you from doing homework.	Do you work harder in order to stay out of trouble?	Ask another player to tell about what 2 things they want to improve on this year.	Who is a grown up that you do not want to disappoint?	Do you work harder if you know you will get a reward?
PURPLE	Who is the hardest working person in your family?	Do you usually check over your work when you are done?	When you have a job what would be a reward you would want from your boss?	Name someone who shows good behavior even when the teacher isn't watching.	What is your favorite subject and what is the subject that you are best at?	When you get older, what are 2 careers that you might want.
BLACK	What is your favorite reward at home?	What consequence at home works best to keep you on good behavior?	What are 2 things that motivate you?	Say out loud, "I am pretty awesome!"	Why is it important for doctors to try their best?	Do you get more motivated by sweet treats or free time?

Activity 2.7 – Work Ethic

Activity 2.8 – Good to Great

Name_____

Directions: Think about skills that you are good at. Then, write two statements describing what you would need to do to become great at that skill.

From Good to Great

I am good at:

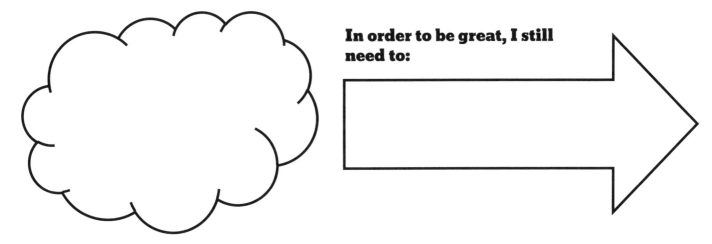

In order to be great, I still need to:

I am good at:

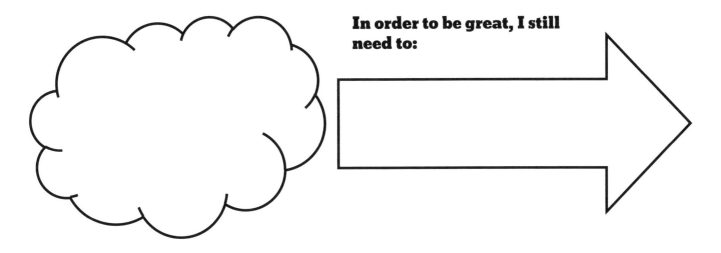

In order to be great, I still need to:

Activity 2.9 – Step 1, 2, 3 Goal: Build a Snowman

Overview: This lesson is a simple way to teach kids about goal setting using the image of building a snowman to create a visual organizer.

ASCA National Competencies Addressed:
- Demonstrate the motivation to achieve individual potential
- Demonstrate how interests, abilities and achievement relate to achieving personal, social, educational and career goals

Material/Resources: Stuffed snowman or poster of a snowman with the word "goal" on his hat, soccer ball, three snowballs with magnet backs, worksheets.

Procedures:
1. Introduce a snowman (either a stuffed animal or a print out of clipart). He likes to play soccer. Discuss a goal in soccer vs. goal in life.

2. Put your thumb up if you know what a soccer goal is (put your thumb sideways if you kind of know, and thumb down if you do not know.) Put your thumb up if you know what a goal in school/life is (put your thumb sideways if you kind of know, and thumb down if you do not know.)

3. Ask students, "What are some goals that you have?"

4. Discuss that having a belief in oneself is an important foundation for any goal.

5. Have class pretend to make a snowman in front of themselves. Ask how they started. (on the bottom and worked up to the hat .. the goal). Have them repeat "Step One, Step Two, Step Three, Goal".

6. Have volunteers create the snowman out of magnet backed circles that counselor/teacher has brought in. Repeat process (with this) in reaching a goal.

7. Have students reach their goal of going back to their seats quietly. Brainstorm some goals and handout worksheet.

8. Instruct students that they should write their sentences first and then can color their snowman (optional; they can draw the snowman achieving their goal.)

Activity 2.9a – Worksheet

Activity 2.10 – Famous Failures

Overview: Work Ethic means trying, and trying again… the people in the first poster did just that, and students will learn through this activity that they did not come by their success without adversity.

ASCA Competencies Addressed:
- Demonstrate the motivation to achieve individual potential
- Demonstrate how interests, abilities and achievement relate to achieving personal, social, educational and career goals

Material/Resources: Copies of worksheet 2.10 (page 73), markers/crayons, small box labeled SELF-TALK (jewelry box, Altoids tin, small Chinese delivery box) slips of paper that say "you can do it," "don't give up!"

Procedures:

1. Ask students "What is self-talk?" Define self-talk as the words we say to ourselves quietly in our heads. There is positive and negative self-talk.

2. Use the small box as a visual. Place box on head and say this is the self-talk in your brain. If you have good work ethic you need this voice of an encouraging coach to remind you that you need to keep trying. Pull out slips of paper to give examples of statements of positive self-talk. (You can do it! Keep Trying!)

3. Use Worksheet 2.10a "Famous Failures" as a prompt for a discussion about how people fail before they succeed.

4. Have students split up into groups of two or three. Print out poster for each group.

5. Have each group discuss the self-talk that must have gone through the celebrity's head when they failed and then how they prevailed and persevered.

6. Assign each group one of the celebrity icons to discuss in front of the class and also discuss what their self-talk might have been.

7. Allow students to color worksheet and teacher can display the best one.

8. Option: Have groups cut out their celebrity and glue it to another piece of construction paper. Below they can either write a paragraph about how they succeeded or write phrase of positive self-talk they might have used.

Activity 2.10 – Famous Failures

Sometimes Failure is Merely Just a First Attempt In Learning!

First Attempt In Learning

WALT DISNEY WAS TOLD THAT HE WAS UNIMAGINATIVE BY A NEWSPAPER FROM WHICH HE WAS FIRED.

Albert Einstein didn't speak until he was 4 years old, and his teachers never thought he would amount to anything.

OPRAH HAD A BOSS THAT AT ONE TIME TOLD HER THAT SHE JUST WASN'T RIGHT FOR TV.

The Beatles were fired by a record company that told them that they had no future in show business.

Michael Jordan was cut from his high school basketball team.

Beethoven's music teacher once told him that he had no chance as a composer.

Poster – The Road to Success

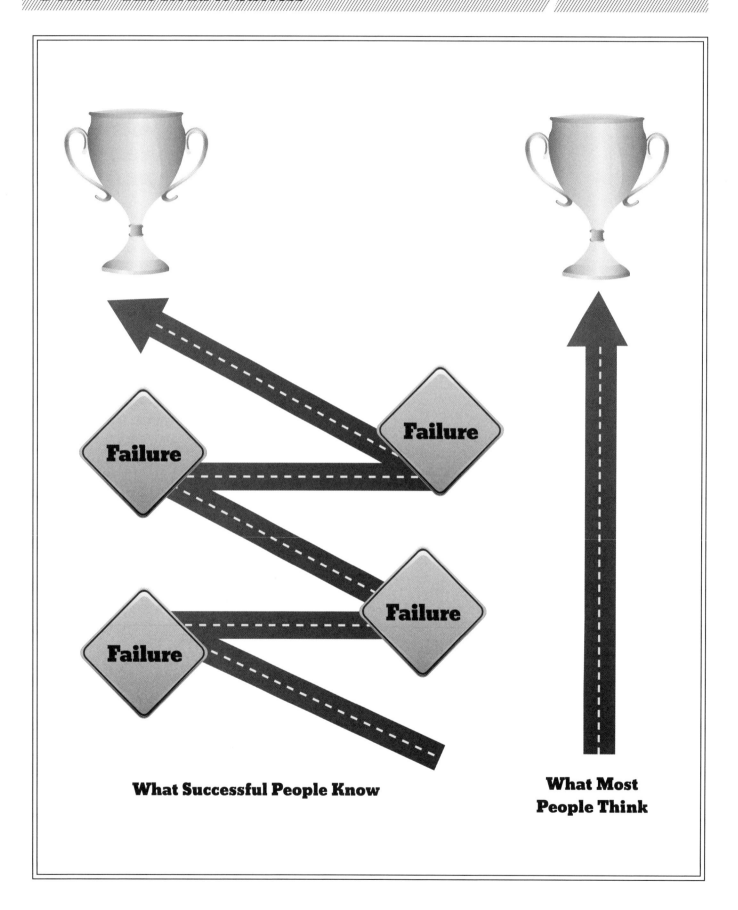

Chapter 3: Self-Control

"A smart person knows what to say. A wise person knows when to say it." – source unknown

ASCA Competencies addressed in this chapter:
- Identify Attitudes and behaviors which lead to successful learning
- Take responsibility for their actions
- Understand the need for self-control and how to practice it
- Demonstrate cooperative behavior in groups
- Learn to work cooperatively with others as a team member
- Learn techniques for managing stress and conflict

Chapter Introduction
Delay of gratification is a difficult concept for kids to grasp, but an essential skill for success. There are many ideas in this chapter to help students understand what it means to stop and think before acting.

Activity	Page #	Chapter Contents
3.0	76	Literature Link
3.1	77	Counselor Connection Card
3.2	78	Word Jumble
3.3	79	On the Job Self-Control Role Plays
3.4	81	Coffee Filter Thoughts
3.5	84	Gimme 5 ways of Deep Breathing
3.6	86	Circle of Control
3.7	88	Stop and Think Willow
3.8	91	Self-Control Dough
3.9	92	'Just Right' Meter
3.10	94	Teacher Pre post for small group

Activity 3.0 – Literature Link: Self-Control

Below are books that will correlate with self-control. There is a line before each book so that you can mark where it is located, so that if you decide to use it in a lesson you know where to find it. (Personal Library, Media Center, online audiobook, Public Library, or Need to Order it)

_____ ***My Mouth is a Volcano by Julia Cook*** – This is an entertaining story of interrupting while others are speaking. It is a positive way to address this behavior and students can relate to this and try to control their mouth from "erupting."

_____ ***Oh No George by Chris Haughton*** – This book takes a realistic look at the impulses of a dog that students can relate to. The repeating theme creates anticipation that is effective for a read aloud. A great lead in or closing story for a lesson on self-control.

_____ ***Lacey Walker Non-Stop Talker by Christianne Jones and Robert Watson*** – This is a great story about listening because Lacey loses her voice. Her silence forces her to be a listener and lots of good things happen because she is quiet.

_____ ***You are a Lion by Taeeun Yoo*** – This book is a wonderful introduction to yoga which is great for kids because it helps with flexibility, focus and relaxation. The author encourages readers to pretend to be the animal: to flutter like a butterfly, hiss like a snake or roar like a lion.

_____ ***Can't Wait Willow by Cindy Ziglar*** – Willow is excited that the circus has finally come to town; she can't wait. The problem is that she can't say no to things that distract her on the way. She learns a valuable lesson about self-control and decision making. See lesson on page 88.

_____ ***Mrs. Gorski I have the Wiggly Fidgets by Barbara Esham*** – David doesn't know how he always ends up in trouble. He comes up with a cure for his wiggle fidgets that he shares at his parent-teacher conference, that may help others with the wiggle fidgets.

_____ ***In One Ear Out the Other by Michael Dahl*** – Listening for Bud doesn't go well. Everything goes in one ear, and out the other. What will his parents do to fix this problem?

_____ ***Interrupting Chicken*** - A little chicken is known for always interrupting stories. Bedtime stories always end when she put in her own ideas. She finally learns her lesson when she tries to tell a story and realizes that someone isn't listening.

Activity 3.1 – Self-Control: Counselor Connection Card

Directions: After a lesson on Self-Control is taught, give each student a copy of the counselor connection card below. If they bring it back by a designated date, they are eligible to win a prize. You can draw three of the counselor connection cards that have been returned and those students are given a prize.

Counselor Connection Card: Self-Control

This week in our counselor's lesson, we reviewed self-control, or stopping and thinking things through before acting. Kids learn best by watching the adults around them. Talk to your child about what issues you have had with self-control in the past and present. Discuss what you have done to help use self-control. Also, ask your child what they do as a "professional student" to use self-control.

Signing this Counselor Connection Card means you have discussed with _____ why having self-control is important.

Student Name _____
Homeroom _____
Adult Signature_____

Counselor Connection Card: Self-Control

This week in our counselor's lesson, we reviewed self-control, or stopping and thinking things through before acting. Kids learn best by watching the adults around them. Talk to your child about what issues you have had with self-control in the past and present. Discuss what you have done to help use self-control. Also, ask your child what they do as a "professional student" to use self-control.

Signing this Counselor Connection Card means you have discussed with _____ why having self-control is important.

Student Name _____
Homeroom _____
Adult Signature_____

Counselor Connection Card: Self-Control

This week in our counselor's lesson, we reviewed self-control, or stopping and thinking things through before acting. Kids learn best by watching the adults around them. Talk to your child about what issues you have had with self-control in the past and present. Discuss what you have done to help use self-control. Also, ask your child what they do as a "professional student" to use self-control.

Signing this Counselor Connection Card means you have discussed with _____ why having self-control is important.

Student Name _____
Homeroom _____
Adult Signature_____

Counselor Connection Card: Self-Control

This week in our counselor's lesson, we reviewed self-control, or stopping and thinking things through before acting. Kids learn best by watching the adults around them. Talk to your child about what issues you have had with self-control in the past and present. Discuss what you have done to help use self-control. Also, ask your child what they do as a "professional student" to use self-control.

Signing this Counselor Connection Card means you have discussed with _____ why having self-control is important.

Student Name _____
Homeroom _____
Adult Signature_____

©YouthLight

Activity 3.2 – Self-Control: Word Jumble and Riddle

Name _____

Directions: Solve each word jumble below. Then after you solve each one, use the number guide to figure out the answer to the riddle. All of the words below have to do with using self-control!

LSEF CNTOLRO   ___ ___ ___ F   C ___ ___ ___ ___ ___ ___
                                                          6

NIATECEP   P ___ ___ ___ ___ ___ ___ ___
                           8

TLAKIGN   ___ ___ ___ ___ ___ ___ G
                     11

INTUPERT   I ___ ___ ___ ___ ___ ___ ___
                            10   2

DATIEW   ___ A ___ ___ ___ ___
            9

IETSNL   ___ ___ S ___ ___ ___
            1

UCOFS   ___ O ___ ___ ___

IDNM   ___ ___ N ___
          7   3

OCSHLO   S ___ ___ ___ ___ ___
              4   5

Riddle: Why is the sun so bright?

Answer:

___ ___ ___ ___ ___ ___ ___ ___ ___ ___ ___ ___ ___ ___ ___
 1   2   3   1   3   1   2   4   5   6   7   8   9   6 10 11

Answer Key to Riddle: IT DID ITS HOMEWORK

78 • ©YouthLight

Activity 3.3 – On the Job Self-Control: Role Plays

Overview: Regardless of what specific career a person chooses, it will require self-control. In the activity below, students will participate in role-plays and then the actors/volunteers will show different types of deep breathing (or other stress relief technique) in order to stop and think.

ASCA National Competencies Addressed:
- Identify Attitudes and behaviors which lead to successful learning

Materials: Role-play cards (page 80), props that help with stress reduction

Procedures:
1. Introduce the lesson by discussing the meaning of self-control.
2. Split the class into groups.
3. Distribute a role-play card to each group. (Copy 3.3A role play cards on page 80)
4. Explain to class that we will be in groups for only 10 minutes and the skits should be no more than one minute. In each skit, the group should show how a worker would have to use a stress reduction technique to help them to stop and think.
5. To begin the skit the facilitator will say, "1,2,3 Action" similar to how a director would in Hollywood. Encourage the students to clap when you say action
6. Practice "1,2,3 Action" (with everyone clapping in unison when "Action" is said.)
7. One person from the first group introduces their group and the counselor leads the class in saying "1,2,3 Action" to signal the group to perform. Subsequently, other groups perform.
8. After the skits, the facilitator leads a discussion asking these questions:
   - What strategy did you use to show self-control?
   - Why is it important to show self-control on the job?

Activity 3.3a – On the Job Self Control Role Play Cards

A surgeon has an itch but he/she has to focus on the important foot surgery he/she is doing.

A teacher had a very bad morning and still has to teach math class.

A customer yells at the cashier and the cashier has to keep calm and not yell back or be rude.

A hair stylist has a party she is excited to go to, but she has to take the time to give her customer a good haircut instead of rushing.

A bus driver is getting frustrated with the students on the bus being loud. The bus driver needs to concentrate on driving.

A waitress is hungry but has to serve customers their food. Although it is tempting to take a few French fries from the customer's plate, he/she uses self-control.

Activity 3.4 – Coffee Filter Thoughts

Overview: This object lesson lets students visualize why filtering thoughts is important. A craft is included using a coffee filter that allows students to have a take home project.

ASCA National Competencies Addressed:
- Understand the need for self-control and how to practice it
- Learn techniques for managing stress and conflict

Materials: Coffee Filter, Colander, Rice, bowl, Worksheet page 83, Scenario Cards (page 82), strips of paper (For optional craft: coffee filter (1 per student), markers, spray water bottle)

Procedures:

1. Show students a colander and a coffee filter. Ask students, "What are these things?"

2. After establishing that these are filters, pour the rice through the colander showing that some of the grains fall through. Ask students to imagine the grains of rice are your thoughts. If you have mean or angry thoughts, do you want them coming out? Not usually.

3. Show premade signs (using worksheet 3.4b) "What you are thinking." versus "What you actually say," and discuss that what we think should not always be what comes out of our mouth.

4. Review that we need to filter our words before we say them out loud. Some people have a filter with large holes like a colander. These people blurt out whatever they think without thinking how those words might affect others. Ask your students what the long term effect might be if you have a colander with large holes? (Answers: very few friends, arguments with other students, tattling, and no one to play with at recess)

5. Others have practiced the skill so their filter is like a coffee filter. These people choose their words carefully and they choose the right time to express their opinion. They use the correct tone, and use the correct words so the other person can "hear" the message. What is the long term effect of having a filter like a coffee filter? (Answer: friends, someone to play with at recess, happiness).

6. Remind your students that if you don't have anything nice to say, don't say anything at all.

7. Use the large colander to show when a thought goes through your head how it should come out. Sometime the thought in your head should stay in your head and nothing comes out.

Activity 3.4 – Coffee Filter Thoughts

Scenario Cards for Activity 3.4

Scenario Card #1:

A new boy has joined your class. His family recently moved here from another country. He speaks with an accent.

Wrong way: "You talk funny."

Right way: "Where did you live before you moved here? Did you speak a different language? That's great! Can you teach me a few words?"

Scenario Card #2:

Jake just got his first pair of glasses. He is nervous about going to school because he thinks the other students will make fun of him.

Wrong way: "I'm glad I have good eyesight because those glasses make you look dumb!"

Right way: "Hi Jake! Cool glasses! My friend has some like those. He told me that his grades improved after he got them."

Optional Craft to Support Lesson:

3.4a Sailboat Filter Craft:

1. Students should color coffee filter using different colors - the more area they color the more vibrant your colors will be.

2. Using a spray water bottle, spray water directly onto the coffee filter. Try not to overspray the filter – a little water goes a long way with this. The colors will mix with each other.

3. Let coffee filter dry – this doesn't take too long since they are thin.

4. Glue coffee filter to sail template.

Activity 3.4a – Worksheet

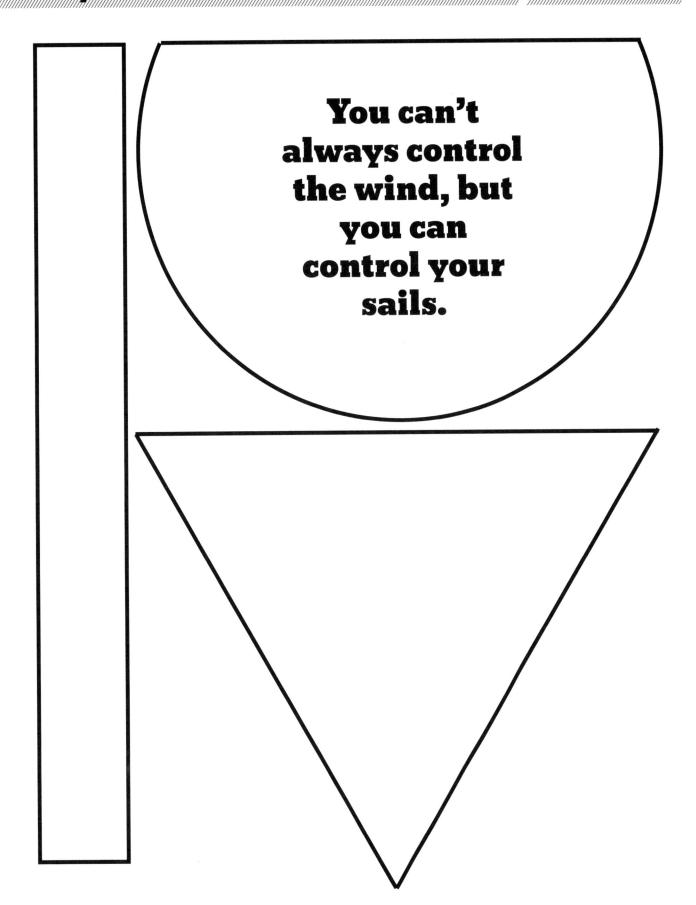

You can't always control the wind, but you can control your sails.

Activity 3.5 – Give me Five Ways of Deep Breathing

Overview: This lesson reviews different techniques of deep breathing.

ASCA National Competencies Addressed:
- Student will learn to demonstrate dependability, productivity and initiative.
- Learn techniques for managing stress and conflict

Materials: Worksheet 3.5a on page 85, scratch and sniff stickers, candle, bubbles, Supplement with YouTube video: Belly Breathe

Procedures:

1. Ask the students to take 3 deep breaths. Then tell them that most of them did it "wrong." Explain, that it is not really wrong, but just not the most effective deep breath. Some people were even hyperventilating which doesn't calm people down at all. Today we will learn how to take deep breaths as a method of calming down and getting the most oxygen to our brain as possible, so we can make good decisions.

2. Teach the following deep breathing techniques. The purpose here is to not just breathe, but to help students learn to breathe s-l-o-w-l-y.

   - Belly Breathing – breathing in deep enough to focus on expanding that belly (YouTube video on Belly Breathing available with Elmo)
   - Snake breathing-focusing on breathing out slowly, using a hissing sound
   - Flower/Candle: Smell a flower, then Blow out the candles
   - Choo Choo Breathing. (Breath in slowly, and then out in 3 Choo's (Choo, choo, choo)
   - Blow Bubbles
   - Square Breathing: Make a square with your hand in the air. Breathe in while your hand is on top. Hold your breath while moving your hand down, and let is out while you move your hand to the bottom and up again. (So in for one side, hold for one side, out for two sides of the square.)
   - Press Breathing with 4-4-4 (Put hands together and while pressing count in for 4, hold for 4, and out for 4).

3. After teaching all of these methods, distribute worksheet 3.5 to students and have them choose 5 to write out on the hand worksheet.

4. As a post lesson evaluation, students can rotate around the room and share favorite ways of breathing. Compare with each other which one is your favorite.

Activity 3.5a – Worksheet

Name _____

Directions: Choose 5 different ways to take a deep breath that you think would work for you. Color in the two ways you think will work best.

GIVE ME 5: Different Ways of Taking a Deep Breath

Self-Control

| Choo Choo Breathing | Belly Breathing | Flower Candle Breathing |
| Blow Bubbles | Square Breathing | Press Breathing |

4-4-4

©YouthLight • 85

Activity 3.6 – Circle of Control

Overview: Part of having self-control is understanding that YOU are in control of your behaviors.

ASCA National Competencies Addressed::
• Student will learn to demonstrate dependability, productivity and initiative.

Materials: Hoola hoop, index cards labeled with things such as: having good manners, rainy days, helping people, barking dogs, being happy.

Procedures:

1. Bring in a hoola hoop. Ask students what this is? When they answer "hoola hoop" tell them that today we are going to call this something different, we will call it the circle of control.

2. Discuss with students that there are some things in life that are outside of your control and some things that you can control, that are in the Circle of Control.

3. Give examples, on the board: having good manners, rainy days, helping people, barking dogs, and being happy.

4. Instruct the students to decide if it is something they have control over (inside the hoola hoop) or something they do not have control over (outside the hoola-hoop).

5. Have a student volunteer to put cards labeled with ideas either inside or outside the hoola hoop to demonstrate.

6. Distribute worksheet 3.6a (on page 87) to students. Have them complete this (either individually or in pairs)

7. Remind students that their effort IS within their circle of control.

8. After students complete this activity, they can write words on cards of other concepts that are either in their control or not and have them put them in the appropriate place in or out of the hoola hoop.

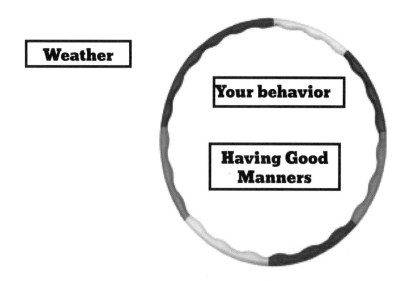

86 • ©YouthLight

Activity 3.6a – Circle of Control

Name _____

Directions: Cut out the squares below and use a glue stick to put them in the appropriate place. Are they in your circle of control or outside??

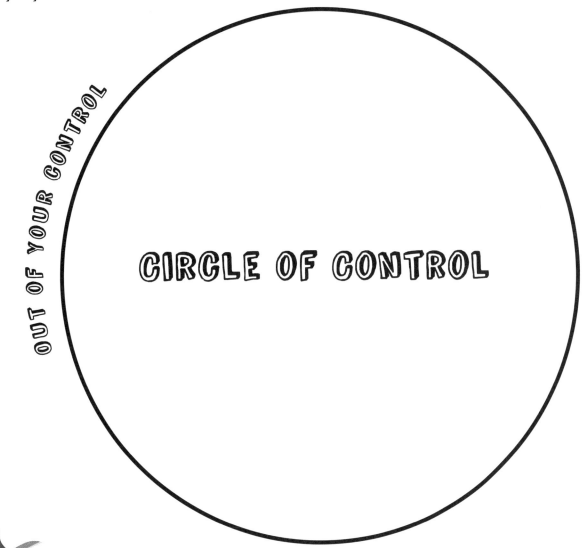

OUT OF YOUR CONTROL

CIRCLE OF CONTROL

Having good manners	A Snow Storm	A dog in your neighborhood barking	A traffic jam
Calling out in class	Brushing your teeth	Finishing your homework	What game you play during recess.
Studying for a spelling test	Your parent's behavior	What is served for lunch in the cafeteria	A classmate is mean to you

©YouthLight • 87

Activity 3.7 – Stop and Think Willow!

Overview: This lesson gives students the definition of what self-control is, but also a story to give context, and an activity to make their own stop and think visual for their desk.

ASCA National Competencies Addressed:
- Student will learn to demonstrate dependability, productivity and initiative.

Materials: Bubbles to use, *Can't Wait Willow* by Cindy Ziglar, one stop sign make and take for each student (see Activity 3.7b on page 90), bubbles to give away (optional)

Procedures:

1. Ask the class, "Do you like Bubbles?" Of course they will all say yes. Tell students that you will blow bubbles over their heads and the only rule is no popping the bubbles and no calling out.

2. After doing this, tell the students that the feeling that they had when they wanted to pop the bubbles but didn't do it… is called self-control. It is when you have the impulse/desire to do something but you stop and think.

3. Show students the motions for stop and think (Touch your brain and then hold out your hand out in a stop gesture.) Tell students that during this lesson I might do that motion to you if you need to stop and think and use self-control. Your teacher might also use this in class.

4. Show class poster on page 89. Tell the students that we need to train and workout the brain just like we do our muscles. How many times will someone need to lift weights to have a strong muscle (100's). We have to work out our brain the same way. Practice 100's of times.

5. Now we will read a book called *Can't Wait Willow* about a little girl who is trying to learn to use self-control. As I am reading, show me the hand signal for stop and think each time Willow should use self-control. I will be watching to see who "gets it".

6. After reading story ask what Willow learned. She learned to stop and think. Present each student with a stop sign from page 90 and show them a sample that you have decorated. Tell them that they can tape this to their desk/table or they can punch a hole in it and make it into a necklace or door hanger.

Supplement/Extension:

I bring in a puppet of a dog named Impulsive Puppy to start out this lesson. I tell the students that he used to have a problem sticking his tongue out at students (all the while manipulating the puppet to stick out his tongue at people.) Once the students yell out, "He is sticking his tongue out now!" I then put Impulsive Puppy in time-out and have him watch for good listeners. Also, I sometimes give him a "stop and think necklace."

Activity 3.7a – Poster

Self-Control:

Build up your muscle!

Activity 3.7b

Directions: Have students write the word "THINK" in the word bubble and then color in the stop sign. These can be made into necklaces or laminated to put on student desks.

Activity 3.8 – Self-Control Dough

Overview: Give students a tangible stress management tool and discuss the power of self-talk as a way to practice self-control.

ASCA National Competencies Addressed:
- Understand the need for self-control and how to practice it
- Learn techniques for managing stress and conflict

Materials: Mini cans of play dough for each student, markers, strips of paper to label the mini play dough

Procedures:
1. Buy enough mini party size play-dough for each student. (You can buy an 8 pack at various dollar stores, so it really is affordable).
2. Review self-control techniques (also known as stress relievers or anger management techniques). List; deep breathing, playing outside, talking to friends, etc. Include in the list of techniques, to use or squish play-dough.
3. Also, define and brainstorm some positive affirmations and list them on the board or a piece of paper.
4. Have students decorate a label for their "Self-Control Dough." They can either choose a label below to color in, or they can use a blank piece of paper and write out several of the brainstormed affirmations or ideas of what to do when stressed.
5. Students can take play dough home. (This is a great lesson to do around standardized testing!)

Optional use of play dough for individual and group counseling sessions:
After students decorate their play dough can, ask students to think of an animal. Once each student has an animal in mind, instruct the students to mold the animal out of Play-dough. After everyone has created an animal, students share what they created and how that animal's personality is like their own.

Activity 3.9 – Just Right Meter

Don't give up what you want most, for what you want now.

Overview: Create a meter so that students can self-monitor their level of control.

ASCA National Competencies Addressed::
- Understand the need for self-control and how to practice it
- Demonstrate cooperative behavior in groups
- Learn techniques for managing stress and conflict

Materials: Small label stickers, metal brads, paper plates (preferably small), markers

Procedures:

1. Distribute paper plates cut in half to each student. (As a prep activity and time saver, stencil/separate the plate into thirds in pencil.)

2. Tell students that we will be making "Just Right" meters today to help us stay in control of ourselves. Sometimes we don't realize that we are too loud, too angry, or too lazy. It happens to everyone. This meter will help us monitor ourselves.

3. Have students color each section a different color.

4. On small labels (or directly on the plate) write "not enough," "just right," and "too much." Label each section appropriately.

5. Apply arrow in the center with brad so that the arrow can rotate to each section.

6. Use this meter to display things like volume, proximity in talking, energy level.

Activity 3.9 Just Right Meter

Other Ideas

Self-Control Cubes

You can use self-control cubes* as an incentive in small groups. Simply give students a self-control cube for any positive behavior. At the end of group, whichever student has the most cubes, gets to go to the treasure box. *(Any small chips or cubes will work. Seen here are small counter cubes in a recycled creamer plastic carton.)

Self-Control Bubbles

Bubbles are a great metaphor to help kids know what using self-control feels like. To demonstrate this, blow bubbles over the heads of your students. Watch as they pop the bubbles instinctively. Next, tell the students that this time when you blow the bubbles towards them they are not allowed to pop the bubbles. After doing this, tell the student that the feeling of wanting to pop the bubbles but not popping them is using self-control. (Show image on Poster 3.7a)

Activity 3.10 – Self-Control Group

Teacher Pre/Post Form

Teacher: _____ Student: _____

Please fill out the following checklist to help me understand your student better. Please add any helpful information at the bottom of the page. This information will be used to determine the members and content of the Self-Control Small Group.

	Strongly Agree	Agree	Disagree	Strongly Disagree
Student is aware of his/her distractibility.				
Student is able to filter out distractions to stay on task.				
Student can stop and think of a plan before acting.				
Student is aware of the consequences of his/her actions.				
Student learns from his/her mistakes.				
Student is able to calm him/herself down in situations (whether upset or too active)				
Student seeks appropriate help when problem-solving.				
Student can easily overcome struggles.				

Briefly, what do you hope this student learns in the Focus Small Group?

_____

_____

Circle for the following:

Math: On grade level   Below grade level   Above grade level

Reading: On grade level   Below grade level   Above grade level

Conduct grades: _____

Chapter 4: Teamwork

Teamwork divides the task and multiplies the success!

ASCA Competencies addressed in this chapter:
- Learn to work cooperatively with others as a team member
- Learn how to interact and work cooperatively in teams.
- Acquire employability skills such as working on a team, problem-solving and organizational skills
- Demonstrate cooperative behavior in groups

Chapter Introduction
No matter what type of job you have, you have to get along with others. The ability to work successfully with a team is an essential skill for school and career. While it isn't always easy to work with others, it is one of the most important characteristics that employers seek out.

Activity	Page #	Chapter Contents
4.0	96	Literature Link
4.1	98	Counselor Connection Card
4.2	99	Teamwork Poem
4.3	101	Teamwork Cryptogram Activity
4.4	106	Don't Lose your Marbles Teamwork Game
4.5	107	Play Dough a la Teamwork
4.6	109	Career Cluster Showdown
4.7	111	Teamwork: Being a piece of the Puzzle
4.8	116	Crayon Box Activity

Activity 4.0 – Literature Link: Teamwork

Below are books that will correlate with self-control. There is a line before each book so that you can mark where it is located, so that if you decide to use it in a lesson you know where to find it. (Personal Library, Media Center, online audiobook, Public Library, or Need to Order it)

_____ ***Michael's Golden Rule* by Deloris Jordan** – Jonathan and Michael are on a baseball team that isn't doing well. Michael's Uncle Jack gives them advice about his golden rule of baseball, that there is more to a good game than winning or losing.

_____ ***Teamwork Isn't My Thing and I Don't Like to Share* by Julia Cook** – In this book, RJ has to learn to get along while doing a group project at school. RJ also struggles with sharing with his sister at home, and a great example is given when they have to share the last cookie in the jar. After a pep talk from his soccer coach, RJ learns a valuable lesson in teamwork that he transfers to school and home.

_____ ***Pumpkin Soup* by Helen Cooper** – Three friends make their pumpkin soup every day in the same way. The Cat slices, the Squirrel stirs, and the Duck puts in the salt. But one day the Duck wants to stir instead which creates a big fight. Duck leaves the cabin upset. Soon, the Cat and the Squirrel start to worry and begin to look for their friend. All students who have had big fights over little things will be able to relate.

_____ ***Game Day* by Tiki Barber** – Written by two NFL superstars, this story is about two brothers that play on the same football team. Tiki has had seven touch-downs this season, and Ronde can't help feeling a little jealous especially since he has lead the way with his blocks. The boys learn to deal with their feelings and work for the team's best interest.

_____ ***Joni and the Fallen Star: Helping Children Learn Teamwork* by Cindi Jett** – Pilon Al, a star from the Big Dipper fell out of the sky. Joni and her classmates each combine their individual special talents (building, math, painting, etc.) to help the little star back into the sky. This is a great book to use in discussion about being stronger when we all work together.

_____ ***Sophie and the Perfect Poem: Habit 6 (The 7 Habits of Happy Kids) Hardcover*** – When the teacher tells the class to write a poem, and everyone has to work in pairs, Sophie is assigned to work with Biff. She is sure it's going to be awful because Biff is mean. As they work together, they find they have things in common and that in working together you can create awesome things.

Activity 4.0 – Literature Link: Teamwork

_____ ***Swimmy* by Leo Lionni** – Swimmy is in the big ocean and is fearful of the big fish of the sea. When Swimmy meets other fish his size, he teaches them to work together to be a strong force.

_____ ***Chopsticks* by Amy Krouse Rosenthal** – This is a story of two chopsticks who have been friends for as long as they can remember. But then one day one of the pair gets hurt and the story explores the importance of independence and the unbreakable bonds of friendship.

_____ ***The Best Colors* by Taff** – This book manages in a unique way to teach two important themes: that all colors are "good" and that there are positive outcomes when we can find ways to overcome conflict and competition. The primary colors compete to be the best when they are surprised to discover friendship and acceptance.

_____ ***Crayon Box that Talked* by Shane DeRolf** - In this rhyming book, the crayons learn about diversity. They realize that they need to work together to do their best work.

_____ ***The Day the Crayons Quit* by Drew Daywalt** – Duncan's crayons have gone on strike. What can he do to make them want to come back to work? Each crayon writes Duncan a letter to express their feelings.

_____ ***Friendship is an ART* by Julia Cook** – This story is about a box of colored pencils. The color Brown finds out that in order to have friends, one has to be a friend. In the end, Brown realizes that once he embraces all of his good character traits he is able to make friends with the other colors.

_____ ***Good Night Good Night Construction Site* by Sherri Duskey Rinker** – In this book, excavators, backhoes, front end loads, bulldozers, all must work together on the construction site. This book is a great way to discuss how all of the vehicles work as a team. (This could segue to a project of creating a class book *Good Night, Good Night Any Workplace Site*.)

Activity 4.1 – Teamwork: Counselor Connection Card

Directions: After a lesson on teamwork is taught, give each student a copy of the counselor connection card below. If they bring it back by a designated date, they are eligible to win a prize. You can draw three of the counselor connection cards that have been returned and those students are given a prize.

Counselor Connection Card: Teamwork

This week in our counselor curriculum lesson, we reviewed the concept of teamwork. Talk to your child about what teams you have been on and how you have handled getting along with others even if you have disagreements. Ask your child what they do as a "professional student" to get along with others at their place of work... their school.

Signing this Counselor Connection Card means you have discussed with _____ why teamwork is important.

Student Name _____

Homeroom _____

Adult Signature _____

Counselor Connection Card: Teamwork

This week in our counselor curriculum lesson, we reviewed the concept of teamwork. Talk to your child about what teams you have been on and how you have handled getting along with others even if you have disagreements. Ask your child what they do as a "professional student" to get along with others at their place of work... their school.

Signing this Counselor Connection Card means you have discussed with _____ why teamwork is important.

Student Name _____

Homeroom _____

Adult Signature _____

Counselor Connection Card: Teamwork

This week in our counselor curriculum lesson, we reviewed the concept of teamwork. Talk to your child about what teams you have been on and how you have handled getting along with others even if you have disagreements. Ask your child what they do as a "professional student" to get along with others at their place of work... their school.

Signing this Counselor Connection Card means you have discussed with _____ why teamwork is important.

Student Name _____

Homeroom _____

Adult Signature _____

Counselor Connection Card: Teamwork

This week in our counselor curriculum lesson, we reviewed the concept of teamwork. Talk to your child about what teams you have been on and how you have handled getting along with others even if you have disagreements. Ask your child what they do as a "professional student" to get along with others at their place of work... their school.

Signing this Counselor Connection Card means you have discussed with _____ why teamwork is important.

Student Name _____

Homeroom _____

Adult Signature _____

Activity 4.2 – Teamwork Poem and Lesson

Procedures:

1. Ask students, "What do a family and a class have in common?" (both are groups of people who work and play together)

2. How many teams/groups are you a part of in your life right now? Stand up if you are in this group:

- Choir or Music
- Brownies/Girl Scouts
- After School Program
- PE class
- Church/Synagogue
- Bus rider
- Dance
- Cub Scouts
- Sport team
- Neighborhood
- Gymnastics
- 3rd grade
- Swim team
- Spelling Bee
- Cheerleading

"Since everyone belongs to so many different groups, it would be nice if everyone got along and worked well together."

3. Choose one of the following activities to do with this poem.

Choice 1: You can work with a partner or with a group to present this poem to the class. Your team/group will have 6 minutes to work on it and then you will present the poem to the entire class. (After 6 minutes have students that were preparing the poem to complete the questions about how they got along in their group.)

Choice 2: Draw a picture of a team that you are on or a team that you would like to be on.

Worksheet 4.2a – Teamwork

From family members and soccer teams

To gymnastics friends on balance beams

Karate pals and fun church groups

Nature clubs and boy scout troops

Classroom groups and talent shows

Having fun and sharing woes

There are lots of groups to which you can belong

Which team helps YOU feel most strong?

Activity 4.3 – Teamwork Cryptogram Activity

Overview: Groups will work on these cryptograms. When the puzzles are solved they will reveal statements about teamwork.

ASCA National Competencies Addressed:
• Learn to work cooperatively with others as a team member.
• Learn how to interact and work cooperatively in teams.

Materials: Worksheets of cryptograms, 3 colors of paper to copy each cryptogram

Procedures:

1. Ask the class why teamwork is important.

2. Before starting the activity, show the students the samples of cryptograms see page 102).

3. Tell students that they will get into groups of 2 or 3 to complete these cryptograms.

4. After students get into their groups, tell students that there are 3 cryptograms (each one on different color paper). Explain that when your team finishes the first color, they come hand it in to me and if correct they will receive the 2nd color/2nd puzzle. And when they are done with the 2nd puzzle they will receive the 3rd. Whichever team finishes with the 3rd puzzle first, wins.

5. As students proceed with the puzzles you can progressively give clues so that the frustration level stays contained.

6. To reward the winners, bring a box of fun pencils. Also, choose 2 students that were not on the winning team, but displayed good teamwork despite frustration to also choose a prize.

Answer to Cryptogram #1: Sticks in a bundle are unbreakable. (Kenyan Proverb)

Answer to Cryptogram #2: "Snowflakes are one of nature's most fragile things, but just look at what they can do when they stick together." (Quote by Vesta M. Kelly)

Answer to Cryptogram #3: Name two reasons that you were able to complete these puzzles.

Activity 4.3a – Teamwork Cryptogram Sample

Directions: This puzzle is called a Cryptogram. At the top there is a KEY that lists all the letters from A thru Z with a box below. Each letter in the puzzle has a number below it; some are already filled in and some you have to figure out. Once you figure out which number goes with a letter, go through the puzzle and every time that number appears, fill in the corresponding letter.

Key:

A	B	C	D	E	F	G	H	I	J	K	L	M	N	O	P	Q	R	S	T	U	V	W	X	Y	Z
			25														13	8	17			11			

Puzzle:

D __ **D**   **W** __   **D** __   **T** __ __   **S**   **R** __ __ __ **T** ?
25 10 25   11 16   25 18   17 20 10   8   15 10 5 20 17

In the sample puzzle above, decide which letter you can figure out. You can probably tell that the letter I goes above the number 10 in the word DID. Since now you know that 10 is I, go through and fill in I above all 10's in the puzzle. That should help you figure out what other letters should be filled in. The other puzzles we will do are figured out in the same way.

Activity 4.3b – Teamwork Cryptogram #1

Directions: This puzzle is called a Cryptogram. At the top there is a KEY that lists all the letters from A thru Z with a box below. Each letter in the puzzle has a number below it; some are already filled in and some you have to figure out. Once you figure out which number goes with a letter, go through the puzzle and every time that number appears, fill in the corresponding letter.

Key:

A	B	C	D	E	F	G	H	I	J	K	L	M	N	O	P	Q	R	S	T	U	V	W	X	Y	Z
				1				4			13		17				6	21	2						

Puzzle:

```
S   T   I   _   _   S       I   N       _       _   _   N   _   L   E       _   R   E
21  2   4   7   20  21      4   17      9       8   22  17  16  13  1       9   6   1

        _   N   _   R   E   _   _   _   L   E  .
        22  17  8   6   1   9   20  9   8   13  1
```

Activity 4.3c – Teamwork Cryptogram #2

Directions: This puzzle is called a Cryptogram. At the top there is a KEY that lists all the letters from A thru Z with a box below. Each letter in the puzzle has a number below it; some are already filled in and some you have to figure out. Once you figure out which number goes with a letter, go through the puzzle and every time that number appears, fill in the corresponding letter.

Key:

A	B	C	D	E	F	G	H	I	J	K	L	M	N	O	P	Q	R	S	T	U	V	W	X	Y	Z
3				26						22	6		23				20	11	7						

Puzzle:

S N _ _ _ L A K E S   A R E   _ N E   _ _
11 23 21 8 24 6 3 22 26 11   3 20 26   21 23 26   21 24

N A T _ R E ' S   _ _ S T   _ R A _ _ L E
23 3 7 16 20 26   11   25 21 11 7   24 20 3 18 1 6 26

T _ _ N _ S ,   _ _ T   _ _ S T   L _ _ K   A T
7 4 1 23 18 11   5 16 7   14 16 11 7   6 21 21 22   3 7

_ _ A T   T _ E _   _ A N   _ _   _ _ E N   T _ E _
8 4 3 7   7 4 26 9   15 3 23   19 21   8 4 26 23   7 4 26 9

S T _ _ K   T _ _ E T _ E R .
11 7 1 15 22   7 21 18 26 7 4 26 20

104 • ©YouthLight

Activity 4.3d – Teamwork Cryptogram #3

Directions: This puzzle is called a Cryptogram. At the top there is a KEY that lists all the letters from A thru Z with a box below. Each of the letters has a corresponding number; some are already shown. Fill in the letters that correspond to the numbers below the blanks to solve the phrase.

Key:

A	B	C	D	E	F	G	H	I	J	K	L	M	N	O	P	Q	R	S	T	U	V	W	X	Y	Z
											6	12	1				9	3	23			15			

Puzzle:

N __ M __   T W __   R __ __ S __ N S   T __ __ T   __ __ __
1 19 12 16 23 15 8   9 16 19 3 8 1 3   23 26 19 23   14 8 18

W __ R __   __ __ L __   T __   __ M __ L __ T __
15 16 9 16 19 24 6 16   23 8   4 8 12 2 6 16 23 16

T __ __ S __   __ __ __ __ L __ S .
23 26 16 3 16 2 18 13 13 6 16 3

Activity 4.4 – Don't Lose Your Marbles Teamwork Game

Overview: Each child is given a paper towel holder cut lengthwise into a long u-shaped tube. Children stand in teams and they pass a marble from one end of the line to the other using only their piece of tube (not their hands). If the marble falls it has to go back to the start of the line again.

ASCA National Competencies Addressed:
- Student will learn to demonstrate dependability, productivity and initiative.

Materials: Marbles, paper towel tubes cut in half lengthwise, several buckets or tubs.

Procedures:
1. Divide class into groups of about 3-5 kids each group.
2. Distribute a long u-shaped piece of cardboard (paper towel roll cut in half lengthwise) to each child.
3. Tell students that each team will receive a marble. The object is to get the marble through everyone's tubes and into a bucket. No one is allowed to touch the marble with their hands and the marble must go through everyone's tube. If the marble falls it has to go back to the first person again. The last person of the team needs to deposit the marble in a bucket.
4. After the game, discuss the fact that they needed to try to keep the marble under control and, if they lost control of the marble, it had consequences for the whole team even if it wasn't on purpose.
5. Compare losing control of the marble to losing control of our emotions and why this is so important in working in a group or team. Ask students if they got frustrated with each other? If so, did you yell at your teammates or just keep it in your head. Not only is keeping the marble under control difficult, so is keeping your thoughts to yourself, but this is part of teamwork.

TIP: Send out a message to staff that you are collecting paper towel rolls, and you will be amazed how many you get!

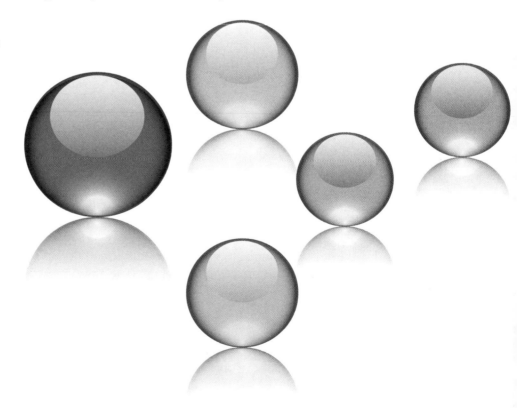

Activity 4.5 – Play-dough a la Teamwork

Overview: This fun and interactive lesson leaves students with a lesson on teamwork, not fighting over simple things, and a bag of play-dough.

ASCA National Competencies Addressed:
- Students will acquire the attitudes, knowledge and skills that contribute to effective learning in school and across the life span.

Materials: *Pumpkin Soup* by Helen Cooper, ingredients for play-dough (see recipe), chef's hat, ziplocs. Story sequencing cards page 108, sign that says "Chef's Table," several mini play-dough, scissors.

Prep for lesson: Get all ingredients lined up (premeasured if you desire) on a table. In gallon Ziploc bags (5 or 6 depending on the size of group) put Worksheet 4.5a (on orange paper optional), two pairs of scissors, and a mini play dough)

Procedures:
1. Wear a chef's hat that says TEAMWORK. Hold up the book and ask the kids (in a French accent for good measure), "What do you think we are learning about today?" Introduce that today's lesson is about linking teamwork to your future. Let's say if you were a chef like me, who would you need to get along with?
2. Let's read this book about teamwork and see what kind of lesson it teaches.
3. Read the book.
4. After reading the book, ask the students if they have ever let a small problem like this turn into a big problem? "I want to stir!" What about problems like… "It's my turn. You cut me. I want the blue scissors"
5. Share with students that we will now be doing 2 teamwork activities.
6. One activity is that students will be separated into small teams to practice teamwork. They will need to cut up the cards and sequence them (worksheet page 108) to retell the story. When they are finished they can play play-dough charades.
7. The other activity will be that the class will be making play dough. It will only be accomplished through teamwork.
8. Have a discussion with class about what will happen if someone gets a job (like mixing the play dough with their hands) and you wish you could have it. Are you going to whine, pout, or pack up your wheelbarrow and stomp into the woods like duck?? No!
9. As teams are working on sequencing, the counselor asks students to come up one at a time for pouring and mixing play-dough, Jobs can also include dividing small portions of orange play dough into snack size Ziploc bags for the kids to take home.
10. Put on hat that says "Chef Teamwork." Ask class if they enjoyed making Play dough a la Teamwork? Encourage them to say it with a French accent for fun.
11. Optional: Get pumpkin shaped cookie cutters and have the students make pumpkin shapes, put a hole in it and when it dries out, kids can make door ornaments.

Activity 4.5 – Worksheet

Play-dough Recipe

> ## Pumpkin Soup Play-dough Recipe
> 2 cups flour
> 1 cups salt
> 4 teaspoons cream of tartar
> 3 Tbsp oil
> orange food coloring (2 parts yellow, 1 part red)
> 1 ½ cups hot water
>
> Heat water in a microwave to near boiling. Mix all ingredients and stir. Add more flour or water until consistency is to your liking.

Worksheet 4.5a – Story Sequencing Cards

Team: Cut out each card and put the cards in the order in which the story happened. Once you have them in order, read the cards out loud to make sure they make sense. Remember works as a team!

The three friends have a fight and Duck leaves.	**Duck decides he wants to stir but Squirrel and Cat tell him "No!"**
Cat and Squirrel can't find Duck either!	**Cat and Squirrel look for Duck together.**
Cat and Squirrel let Duck stir the soup, and they are friends again.	**Duck comes home! Cat and squirrel are so happy to see him.**
Cat, Squirrel and Duck lived together in the white cabin and life was good.	**Cat goes out looking for Duck, but can't find him.**
They head home when they see a light shining in the cabin.	**THE END!**

108 • ©YouthLight

Activity 4.6 – Career Cluster Showdown: Teamwork

Overview: This is a game that can be played to reinforce the concept that no matter where you work, you will need to get along with others. Interestingly, the game forces the students to get along with each other.

ASCA National Competencies Addressed:
- Learn to work cooperatively with others as a team member
- Identify Attitudes and behaviors which lead to successful learning

Materials: Copies of worksheet for each team.

Procedures:

1. Read *Good Night Construction Site* and discuss the different ways the trucks and people get along and work as a team.

2. Tell students that the activity we will be doing will involve working as a team. Give students the words to say to find a group" Can I be on your team?" or "Do you want to be on our team?" Divide students into groups of 4 or 5 students per team (or have them divide themselves into groups). Have students who are struggling to find a group come stand with you and you can find them a team.

3. Distribute a copy of worksheet to each team.

4. Explain the rules to the game. "I will give each team 1 minute to come up with as many answers as possible to the question I ask. Once the time is up, I will say pencils down. I will ask one team to read their answers one by one and if anyone else has that answer everyone with that answer has to cross that off. Your team will get points for any answer that is not crossed off."

5. Let's look at the sample. If the question is "List as many people as possible that a doctor must get along with at work." You and your team will need to brainstorm who these would be.

Next Round:
- Construction Worker
- Teacher
- Chef

Activity 4.6 – Career Teamwork Showdown

No matter what you choose for your career, you will always have to get along with the people around you. Look at the sample and listen to the directions for this game.

Points: _____

Example: List as many careers as possible that a doctor must get along with at work.

1. ~~nurse~~ (if any other group has this all teams cross it off)
2. ~~patients~~
3. receptionist
4. person that wants to sell them medicine

Round 1: List as many people as possible that a _____ get along with at work.

_____
_____
_____
_____
_____
_____
_____
_____
_____
_____

Round 2: List as many people as possible that a _____ get along with at work.

_____
_____
_____
_____
_____
_____
_____
_____
_____

Round 3: List as many people as possible that a _____ get along with at work.

_____
_____
_____
_____
_____
_____
_____
_____
_____
_____

Activity 4.7 – Teamwork: Being a Piece of the Puzzle

Overview: This hands-on activity is fun and clearly makes the point of needing to work as a team.

ASCA National Competencies Addressed:
- Learn to work cooperatively with others as a team member
- Learn how to interact and work cooperatively in teams
- Acquire employability skills such as working on a team, problem-solving and organizational skills

Materials: Book on teamwork (see list on literature link pages 96-97), Copy of handout 4.6a, 4.6b and 4.6c on different color card stock (ie: one red, one blue, one yellow). Paint each puzzle with modge podge and after it dries cut along thick lines, Copies of Handout 4.6D and/or 4.6E (enough for each student)

Procedures:
1. Read teamwork book from Literature Link pages 96-97). If doing this lesson towards the end of the year, emphasize that in the next grade level more group projects and teamwork is needed.

2. After reading the book tell the class that we will now split up into 3 groups. Leader will then hand out puzzle piece of 3 different colors so that the 3 teams can do a group activity where there are premade puzzles painted and with questions/statements that the group will have to answer.

3. Then have each student make their own puzzle with choices of what is written on it. Copy each page on different color card stock. You could even glue it to cardboard.

4. TIP FOR MAKING THE PUZZLE EASIER: When coloring in the words on this puzzle, choose a different color for each word. For example color the first word blue, the second word orange, the third word purple, etc. This will make putting the puzzle back together again an easier task.

Activity 4.7a – Color the Puzzle

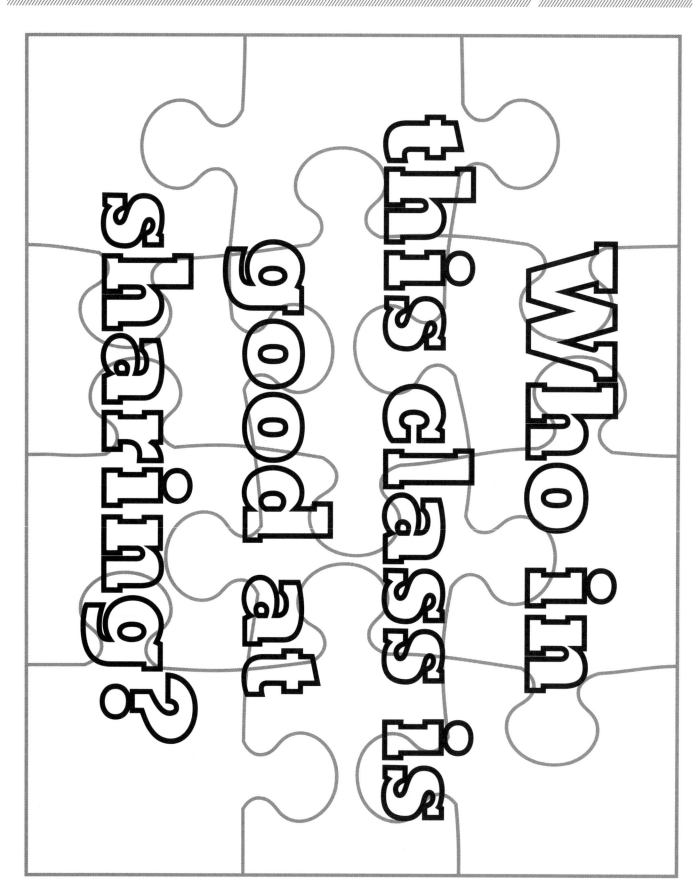

Activity 4.7b – Color the Puzzle

Activity 4.7c – Color the Puzzle

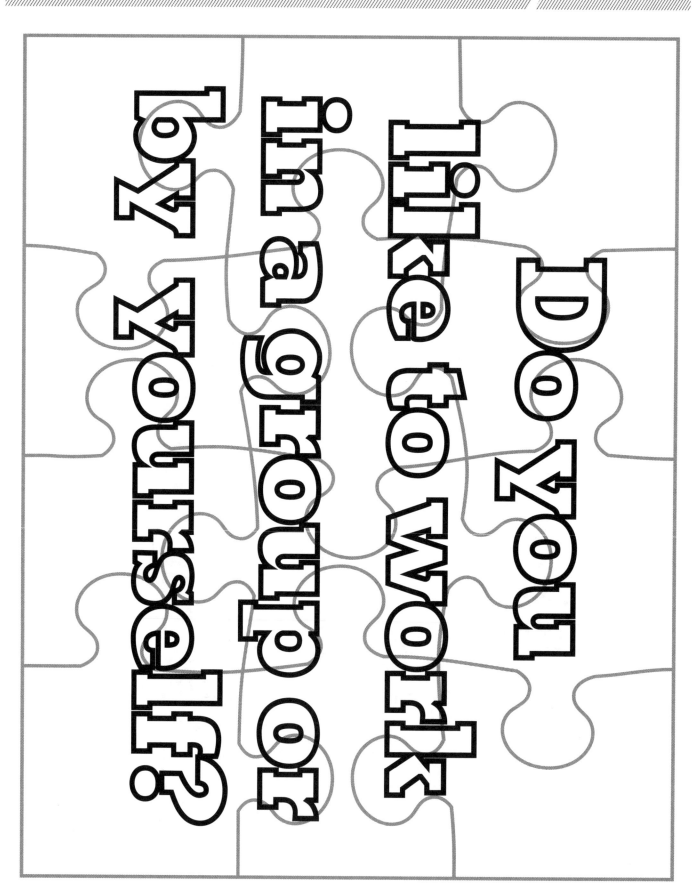

114 • ©YouthLight

Activity 4.7d – Color the Puzzle

Activity 4.8 – Crayon Box Activity

ASCA National Competencies Addressed:
- Demonstrate the ability to work independently, as well as the ability to work cooperatively with other students
- Demonstrate cooperative behavior in groups
- Identify alternative solutions to a problem

Materials: Book of your choice: *Making Friends is an Art* by Julia Cook; *The Crayon Box that Talked* by Shane DeRolf or *The Best Colors by Taff*; 8 boxes of crayons (where there are 8 in a set); Coloring worksheet (enough for every student),

Procedures:
1. Put the same color of crayon in each box. ie: all red in one box.
2. Read *The Crayon Box that Talked* or *The Best Colors* and discuss story with class.
3. Place students in groups of 4 to 8 students. Make sure their desks are cleared of all materials.
4. Give each student a color sheet 4.8A on page 117.
5. Give each table a box of crayons. (If there are only 4 tables, I put the other 4 boxes of crayons on a table in front of the room)
6. Tell students that in this coloring contest these are the rules:
   - Absolutely NO talking.
   - Make your sheet very colorful (Students cannot ask any questions. If they do the questions will not be answered)
7. Tell students that they may begin. Note: When students open the box of crayons they want to ask questions and show you that all the crayons are the same color in their group's box. (I tell them I can't answer any questions, just to do the best that they can. I keep reminding them "No, talking" and "Please make sure your picture is very colorful!")
8. The point of this lesson is for the kids to get up and share. Some students will look around and I verbally will lead them by saying, "Grace is looking around. She is wondering what she can do. The rules are only no talking, the rules don't say anything else." It takes about 5 to 10 minutes before one child will figure out that they can share crayons with the other group without talking. Then, once one child shares, I say, "Look this group has figured it out." I continue to remind them not to talk. Eventually, they will all get up and move around the room borrowing other colors from other groups and then even return them. At the end of the lesson I have them put the crayons in the correct boxes without talking. After the crayons are all in their boxes (same colors together) I give the groups that followed the rules a piece of candy.

Questions to discuss:
1. How did you feel when you saw that the crayons were all the same color?
2. Tell me how you think the world would be different if we were all the same.
3. How can you celebrate your differences with your family, classmates, and friends?

Closing: Differences in people and what we like to do make this world more fun and interesting. Let's celebrate our differences and uniqueness. We can all learn from each other.

Activity 4.8a – Worksheet

Name _____

Colors are the smiles of nature - Leigh Hunt

Chapter 5: Organization

"Clutter is not just the stuff on your floor, it's anything that stands between you and the life you want to be living." – Peter Walsh

ASCA Competencies addressed in this chapter:
- Identify Attitudes and behaviors which lead to successful learning
- Demonstrate dependability, productivity and initiative.
- Acquire employability skills such as working on a team, problem-solving and organizational skills

Chapter Introduction
In today's world of multi-tasking, it is more important than ever to have the organizational skills to keep up with all that needs to be done. In this chapter, there are various activities and lessons that will assist in focusing in on this important skill.

Activity	Page #	Chapter Contents
5.0	119	Literature Link
5.1	120	Counselor Connection Card
5.2	121	Poem
5.3	122	Word Search
5.4	123	Story Connection: Clutter Buster and the Desk Fair
5.5	126	Organization Numbers Game… you gotta have a plan
5.6	128	Organization Relay
5.7	130	Excellence vs. Organization
5.8	132	STAR Students (Students Taking Academics Responsibly)
5.9	133	Organization Centers
5.10	137	Froggy Gets Dressed: Do Things in Order

"Most of employees spend too much time on what is urgent not enough on what is important." – Stephen Covey

Activity 5.0 – Literature Link: Organization

Below are books that will correlate with self-control. There is a line before each book so that you can mark where it is located, so that if you decide to use it in a lesson you know where to find it. (Personal Library, Media Center, online audiobook, Public Library, or Need to Order it)

_____ ***Lazy Daisy* by David Olson** – Daisy likes her messy room with its piles of toys and clothes. Daisy is proud to think of herself as the laziest girl in the world. When Daisy's grandmother gets lost in all the mess, she realizes that keeping things neat has its benefits.

_____ ***The Messiest Desk* by Marty Kelley** – Benjamin has the messiest desk in his class. He has spelling lists from months gone ago, wads of gum, and even some bugs. When he tries to clean his desk, he gets sucked inside. It takes the creativity of the school to save Benjamin from his fate. This rhyming book teaches the benefits of organization.

_____ ***Wyatt Wonder Dog Learns About Being Organized* by Lynn Watts** – Wyatt, a curious dog, decides that he wants to find out more about being organized. He learns his lesson about why it is important to be organized and plan ahead.

_____ ***Messy Melinda* by Nancy Heller** – This is a story of a young girl who is forced to clean up her room. This book shares common thoughts on disorganization, like where to start? In the end, what had been a hard task becomes the source of pride for both Melinda and her mother.

_____ ***The Desk Fairy* by Connie Schnoes** – Did you know that late at night a special visitor comes to your school? The Desk Fairy will encourage your kids to keep their desks organized, by teaching them that it is very rewarding to keep their things neat and clean.

_____ ***A Place for Everything: Habit 3 (The 7 Habits of Happy Kids) Hardcover* by Sean Covey** – Jumper can't find his basketball shoes anywhere and it might be because he is so disorganized. His buddy teaches him the famous words of his father, "A place for everything and everything in its place."

_____ ***Get Organized Without Losing It* by Janet S. Fox** – This book puts useful and pertinent ideas into perspective for older elementary students. It explains the need for being organized and how it can impact other areas of your life. A good one to read together in a small group.

_____ ***Froggy Gets Dressed* by Jonathan London** – Froggy is so excited that it is snowing that he has a hard time remembering what to wear. His mom keeps calling him inside to put on clothes he forgot. This funny story teaches, don't forget to do the first step first, in a funny way. (Of course kids love any story that has the word underwear in it).

_____ ***Zip, Zip ... Homework* by Nancy Poydar** – A great book to help kids who need some help with organization. Violet is excited to have a new backpack to stay organized, but when the homework assignments begin, Violet spends so much time deciding which pocket to use that she accidentally leaves the assignment at school. This book talks about admitting when you are wrong and of course, staying organized.

Activity 5.1 – Organization: Counselor Connection Card

Directions: After a lesson on teamwork is taught, give each student a copy of the counselor connection card below. If they bring it back by a designated date, they are eligible to win a prize. You can draw three of the counselor connection cards that have been returned and those students are given a prize.

Counselor Connection Card: Organization

This week in our counselor's lesson, we reviewed the importance of organizational skills. Kids learn best by watching the adults around them. Talk to your child about how you stay organized (ie: grocery lists, having a place for things to be put away, sorting mail). In your discussion, give an example about some thing that you want to work on organizing better. Also, you can ask your child how they stay organized with all of their chores and assignments.

Signing this Counselor Connection Card means you have discussed with _____ why organization is important.

Student Name _____

Homeroom _____

Adult Signature _____

Counselor Connection Card: Organization

This week in our counselor's lesson, we reviewed the importance of organizational skills. Kids learn best by watching the adults around them. Talk to your child about how you stay organized (ie: grocery lists, having a place for things to be put away, sorting mail). In your discussion, give an example about some thing that you want to work on organizing better. Also, you can ask your child how they stay organized with all of their chores and assignments.

Signing this Counselor Connection Card means you have discussed with _____ why organization is important.

Student Name _____

Homeroom _____

Adult Signature _____

Counselor Connection Card: Organization

This week in our counselor's lesson, we reviewed the importance of organizational skills. Kids learn best by watching the adults around them. Talk to your child about how you stay organized (ie: grocery lists, having a place for things to be put away, sorting mail). In your discussion, give an example about some thing that you want to work on organizing better. Also, you can ask your child how they stay organized with all of their chores and assignments.

Signing this Counselor Connection Card means you have discussed with _____ why organization is important.

Student Name _____

Homeroom _____

Adult Signature _____

Counselor Connection Card: Organization

This week in our counselor's lesson, we reviewed the importance of organizational skills. Kids learn best by watching the adults around them. Talk to your child about how you stay organized (ie: grocery lists, having a place for things to be put away, sorting mail). In your discussion, give an example about some thing that you want to work on organizing better. Also, you can ask your child how they stay organized with all of their chores and assignments.

Signing this Counselor Connection Card means you have discussed with _____ why organization is important.

Student Name _____

Homeroom _____

Adult Signature _____

Activity 5.2 – Worksheet: Organization Poem

A cluttered tornado, my desk is a mess
My disorganization is causing me stress
My homework, a test paper, things my mom signed?
I'm so overwhelmed and always behind.
My skills to keep order and everything stacked
Are broken, and rusty and just out of whack
My teacher does tell me that keeping things straight
Will help my problem of turning things in late
Color coding, and sorting and keeping things clean
Are just not my thing if you know what I mean
What do I do? How do I get started?
Make it a game where I can't get outsmarted?
Start small is the goal and keep things in order
If all goes well, my search will be shorter.

– Lisa King

Draw a picture of a messy desk at school	**Draw a picture of an organized desk**

Activity 5.3 – Organization Word Search

Name _____

Directions: Find the words in the word bank above. Think about how you will go about finding the words. Will you look at one word in the word bank and then look for it? Or will you read all of the words in the word bank and then look for all of them? Will you start from the top and go down or go left to right? Remember that when you have a plan of attack, you will usually do better.

```
C N K I X R T I O A R S T A Z
B A J Q E A P G R S V E C Z B
K X T D I S Y D G U T Q A O C
C A A E O K E R A P E R P D Z
T E P R G K Z N N U Q B L Y Y
L Y T N T O Y Z I J K V A L Z
Q B S Z A H R D Z L H A N T Z
E K K P D G E I E W T N V A G
E F G M Y T P K Z N T U Q E U
A O N L A D B W G E R S O N D
E A R I K S E D O D S G C W U
L Q L F C S P M Z B Q G E L U
D E W I L H E M F P S A M K N
D C L E A N U M R I Z N Y Q X
O Y R Z X E C H J B G Y H V M
```

CATEGORIZE	CLEAN	DESK
DETAILED	LEADER	NEATLY
ORGANIZE	OUTLINE	PLAN
PREPARE	READY	SORT

Activity 5.4a – Organization Story Connection

Overview: Through reading a short story and answering questions, students will understand the importance of staying organized.

ASCA Indicators:
• Student will learn to demonstrate dependability, productivity and initiative.

Materials: Copies of story on page 124 including Discussion Questions on page 125

Procedures:

1. Ask if anyone in the class knows why it is important to be organized.

2. Read story, *Clutter Buster* and the *Desk Fairy,* aloud to the class. Distribute copies if you'd like students to read silently while you read aloud.

3. After they have heard the story, divide the class into groups or pairs.

4. Assign one person in the group to be question reader and one person to be a secretary.

5. After a few minutes, bring the class back together as a whole group and review discussion questions.

6. Tell the class that in the next 2 weeks, the desk fairy just might visit their class and reward students who have a neat desk area. (See handout 5.4B and make copies of this. Counselor should go around to classes within a week of this lesson and tape the certificate and a piece of candy/pencil to their desk).

©YouthLight • 123

Activity 5.4b – Organization Story Connection

Clutter Buster and the Desk Fairy

"Where is it?" Marcus asked. "I know it was here."

His teacher stood over him giving him the look. "Marcus, if you cleaned out your desk, you might actually find your homework. And maybe last night's homework, or your permission slip, book report or agenda."

"I know, I know" he thought, but all he could do was give a deep sigh and say, "I'll clean it". But he didn't really mean it. He wouldn't even know where to start.

Since he didn't have to turn in homework, he had to stay in for recess. "Hmph" he thought. He looked out the window and saw Jenny Jinkins playing with her friends, Jenny always had the matching bows, socks, shirts and skirts. Her desk was just as neat, clean and organized as her clothes. He stared outside and could only say "Hmph."

The next day, when Mrs. Fox's class walked into the room, several students squealed. "OMG!" "Wow!" 4 kids in the class had candy taped to their desk with a note from the "desk fairy." "Hmpph" Marcus thought.

The desk fairy was a new thing that Mrs. Bruster started talking about recently. She said that a fairy came by and checked out everyone's areas and everyone's desk. Sometimes she even left rewards for especially neat students.

Marcus wanted to win a prize, but how could he do it? He knew that his desk, his backpack, even his room was always a mess. Organization was just not his thing. But, at his recess he came up with an idea. Well, actually Jenny Jinkins came up with it.

Several kids were playing a game of chase outside. It started out as Ghost Busters, where Jenny Jinkins was trying to capture the ghosts and zombies, but she changed it up. In the middle of the game she noticed an area of the playground that had trash all over it. She bent down to clean it up and said I have to get this clutter, hold on. Maya and Asher said come on Jenny ... and she said alright, alright. But I have to be a Clutter Buster .... Be careful if you are lying around I will get you too. And she started chasing people saying the Clutter Buster is going to get you.

This got Marcus thinking. Maybe if he was a Clutter Buster in real life, he could figure out how to stay organized. And maybe he could get the Desk Fairy to notice his desk so he could win a prize. He started to pretend he was a Clutter Buster on the playground, copying everything Jenny was doing. Another thought popped into his head. What is he started copying all of the little tricks Jenny was doing in the classroom, like stacking her books neatly, cleaning out her backpack each morning. He started saying Hmmmm .... instead of Hmmph!

When they got back into the classroom, Marcus started his new game of being a Clutter Buster. His teacher Mrs. Fox started to notice. And when he kept this game up at his desk all the next day, the Desk Fairy noticed too.

Activity 5.4c – Worksheet

Discussion Questions:

- Tell me your thoughts about the desk fairy.
- When Marcus copied some of Jenny Jinkins habits what happened to Marcus' work/desk?

Activity 5.5a – Organization Numbers Game ... You Gotta Have a Plan

Materials: Worksheet page 127 (2 copies for each student or one two-sided copy)

Procedures:

1. Distribute one copy of page 127 to the students.

2. Tell the students that they will have 15 seconds to find as many numbers as they can in consecutive order. They must find #1 and circle it then find #2 and circle it, etc.

3. After 15 seconds have passed, tell them to put their pencils down.

4. Ask which student got to the highest number. Ask this student how they accomplished the task. Ask if they had a" method to their madness" or an organized plan?

5. Tell the students that there is a trick. The key to this task is knowing that the best way to do things is usually in an organized way.

6. Have students fold their paper into 4 quadrants (fold it in half vertically, then in half horizontally).

7. Re-open the paper and show the students that there is an organized way to find the numbers. The numbers ascend from quadrant one to two to three to four and then back to one again (so the number 1 and then 5 will be found somewhere in quadrant one.)

8. Allow students to try again when you distribute a second copy of page 127.

9. Discuss how organization helps us to be efficient.

Quadrant 1	**Quadrant 2**
Quadrant 3	**Quadrant 4**

Activity 5.5b – Worksheet

9 1 25 13 17 33 41 29 21 5 37	18 22 6 14 38 30 10 42 26 2 34
19 23 3 31 7 39 27 11 15 43 35	4 16 24 8 28 40 36 12 44 20 32

Copied with Permission from King, L., Academic Advisement. Copyright 2006, Youthlight. Inc. www.youthlight.com

Activity 5.6 – Organization Relay

Overview: In this fun relay race lesson, students will realize that tasks are easier when things are organized.

ASCA National Standard(s):
- Students will acquire the attitudes, knowledge and skills that contribute to effective learning in school and across the life span.

ASCA National Competencies Addressed:
- Improve Academic Self-concept
- Identify attitudes and behaviors that lead to successful learning
- Achieve School Success
- Apply time-management and task-management skills

Materials: 2 boxes/tubs or trays, 30 school supplies (15 different objects: 2 of each. So for instance 2 erasers, 2 pens, 2 calculators, etc.)

Procedures:

1. Enter the classroom with 2 boxes, each filled with 15 different school supplies (the same ones in each box). The objects should be labeled from 1-15 with a sharpie on small labels. The school supplies in one box should be taped down to the box with the numbers pointing up in an orderly fashion. The second box should have the numbered supplies just thrown in there (not taped down or in any order –even turn the numbers upside down to make it more difficult).

2. Put the boxes on opposite sides of the room. Divide the students into 2 teams. It works best to choose about 5 students for each team and let the rest of the class watch. Then, for round 2 you can pick new students. Having a competition between girls vs. boys is also fun.

3. Have each team line up behind their designated box (far enough so they can't see what's in there). Have paper numbered 1 to 15 beside each box. Tell students they will have a relay race and that they have to come up one at a time and find the school supply labeled with number 1 first and then write the name of it on the paper beside number 1. They go to the back of the line and the next person goes up to find number 2. They have to go in order. Tell them that when the last person has gone to tell their team to sit down to determine the winner.

4. Typically, the team with the organized box will win. Tell the losing team that this was a bit unfair to them. Then, I show both teams the other team's boxes. Discuss why the team with the organized box won. I usually show a photo of the two boxes side by side on a PowerPoint and let the students figure out why I knew who would win. Discuss that students always set themselves up to "win" if they are organized.

5. Tell the losing team they will have a chance to redeem themselves and switch the boxes and then play again. Teams should stay in the order they left off so that everyone can have a turn.

6. Discuss how organization can affect their grades (poor grades due to lost homework, etc.) Also discuss how being organized can save them a lot of time to do other things they enjoy. Ask students for examples of things they do to stay organized (for example, getting their book bags ready to go the night before, making checklists, etc.)

Activity 5.6 – Organization Relay

Evaluation: With the time that is left, give them time to clean/organize their desks and tell them that the desk fairy will be visiting sometime soon and will leave a treat for anyone whose desk is still clean and organized. Keep data on the number of students who got a treat.

Activity 5.7a – Excellence vs. Organization

Name _____

Answer the questions below:

Define the word **organization**. Draw a picture and write a definition in your own words. Describe how you can be organized.

Define the word **excellence**. Draw a picture and write a definition in your own words. Describe how you can do things with excellence.

Activity 5.7b – Excellence vs. Organization

Fill in this chart on organization:

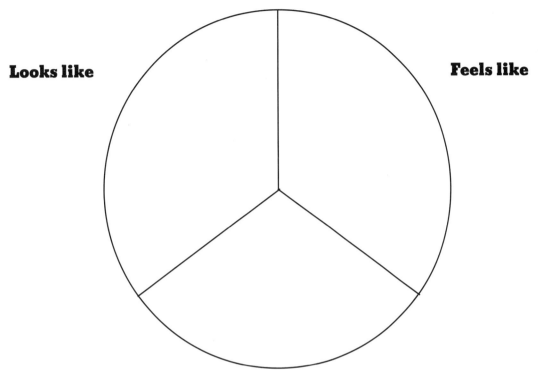

Fill in this chart on excellence:

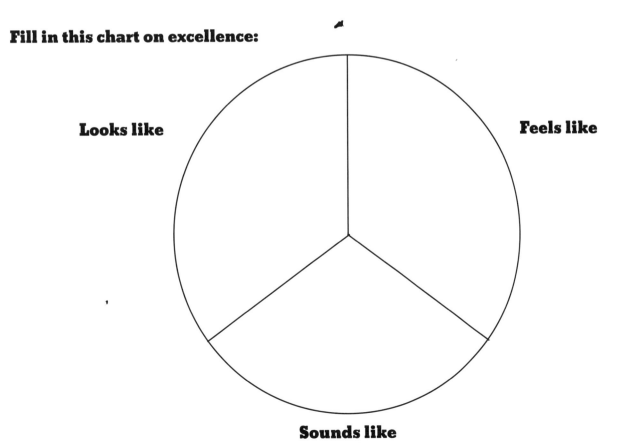

Activity 5.8 – Worksheet

Directions: Write good study tips to decorate your star. You can choose one study tip and write it large and illustrate it, or you can write a study tip in each point of the star.

Some tips that you can decorate your star with:
- Don't procrastinate.
- Keep a list of things you need to do.
- Have an afternoon routine for homework.
- Read every day.
- Clean out your backpack daily.
- Finish homework before free time.
- Set goals for yourself.
- Ask for help if you need it.
- Come up with your own tip to write in.

STAR Students (Students Taking Academics Responsibly)

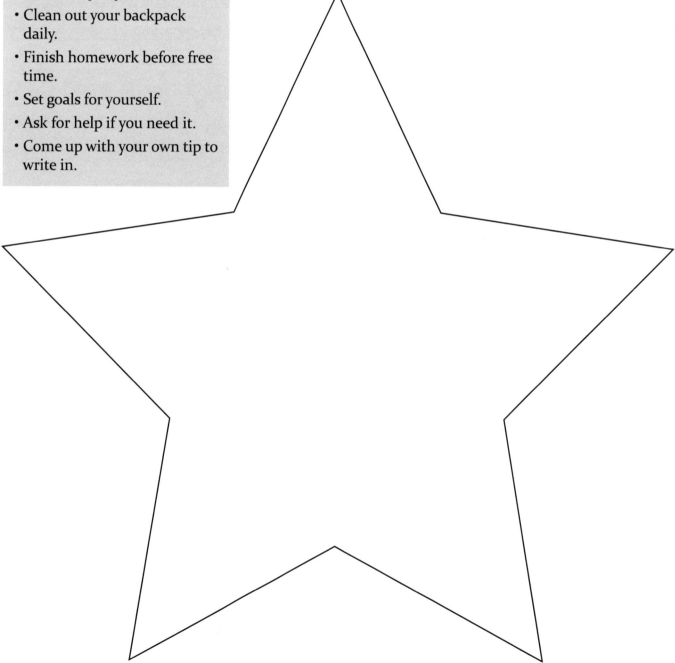

Activity 5.9a – Organization Centers

Preparation:
A center-based lesson can be done in a separate counselor's room if it is large enough, or if there is an empty classroom you can borrow, or centers can be brought into a classroom as mobile centers. Typically, there are 5-6 kids in each group that rotate to each center. Each center lasts about 6 minutes. The counselor rings the bell so that the students know it is time to rotate to the next center.

Sample 30 minute lesson:
Introduction/Explanation of Centers to Whole Class: 4 minutes

To begin, say "Go." Then stop them and say wait we need a plan. Reference that a river might be the same amount of water as a flood (Tim Elmore's theory), but a river is contained and the water knows where it is going. It has a plan. Let's be a river, not a flood. Explain the structure of centers.

Split Students into groups: 1 minute

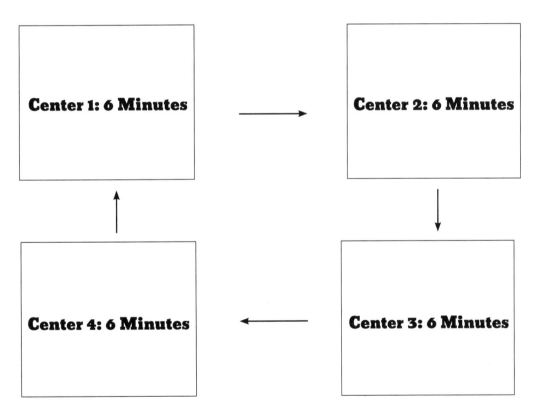

Choose 4 of the following activities (one for each center):
- Make a Bookmark (see page 132)
- Color in the quotes (pages 133-134)
- Mini Lesson on Tips for STAR STUDENTS (page 130)
- Organize Your Socks Activity: Have an assortment of socks in a bin. Have student time each other see how many pairs they can match in 30 seconds.
- Find a suitable video Clip on YouTube, etc. (must be 4-6 minutes for it to work appropriately)
- Silent Reading Center (Choose appropriate books from page 117 to have students read silently)
- Alphabetize Folders
- Word Search (see page 120)

Activity 5.9b – Organization Centers

Decorate bookmark, laminate, punch hole and put yarn through for a great art project for students.

Organization
Make a plan, stick with it! Take it one step at a time!

You don't have to see the whole staircase, just take the first step.
—Martin Luther King Jr.

Organization
Make a plan, stick with it! Take it one step at a time!

You don't have to see the whole staircase, just take the first step.
—Martin Luther King Jr.

Organization
Make a plan, stick with it! Take it one step at a time!

You don't have to see the whole staircase, just take the first step.
—Martin Luther King Jr.

Organization
Make a plan, stick with it! Take it one step at a time!

You don't have to see the whole staircase, just take the first step.
—Martin Luther King Jr.

Activity 5.9c – Mini Posters

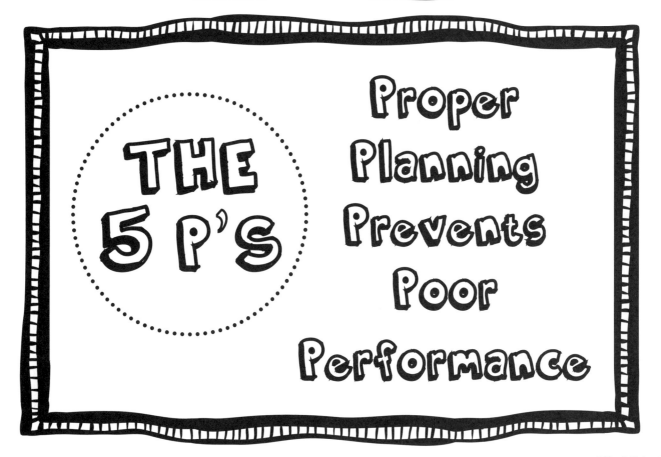

Activity 5.9d – Poster

> # Organizing
> is what you do before you do something, so that when it is done it is not all MIXED UP.
>
> — AA Milne

> # We are what we repeatedly do. Excellence, then, is not an act, but a habit.
>
> — Aristotle

Activity 5.10 – Froggy Gets Dressed Lesson

Overview: Teach students about taking things one step at a time, planning, and accomplishing more when you go one step at a time with this fun lesson that ends with teaching kids to draw a frog in one minute.

ASCA National Competencies Addressed:
• Demonstrate dependability, productivity and initiative.

Materials: *Froggy Gets Dressed* by Jonathan London, A sheet of drawing paper for each student, pencil (and crayons for decorating).

Procedures: (Optional: I put this lesson on powerpoint and hyperlink the Froggy story from YouTube.com. Then, show worksheet 5.10A on the smart board projector.)

1. Introduce that today we will be talking about organization. Ask class the following questions (or show on a powerpoint).
   • Do you think about what you should do first to get started on a task?
   • Do you have a schedule at home (homework, then snack, etc.)?
   • Do you do things right away so that you don't forget to do them?
   • Do you make lists?
   • Do you time yourself to make sure you get things done?

2. Discuss that when you have a lot to do, it helps to think of what is the most important thing to do first, and that is what we will be focusing on today. Tell the children we will be reading a story about a frog that forgot to think of the most important thing first. Organization has to do with remembering things. How can we remember things more easily? (Use examples of teachers lessons plans, I often use PowerPoint to guide my lessons, etc.)

3. One way is to put motions with our words. (This can help you stay organized in studying for tests.) Let's learn some motions that go with this book. Teach the sign language for frog (put back of hand under chin, make a fist and point sideways).

4. Read, *Froggy Gets Dressed* by Jonathan London (a funny way to teach the concept of staying organized).

5. Now that silly story showed that organization has a lot to do with remembering things. Sometimes we remember things by making motions for reminders or visual reminders or (auditory) reminders you hear. Now, let's do an activity to see if visual or auditory reminders work best for you. It's going to be an activity where I will prove to you that you can get more done if you make a plan and start with the first step first.

6. How many of you think you can draw a frog in one or two minutes? Teach how to draw a frog using the guide on worksheet 5.10a.

Activity 5.10 – Froggy Gets Dressed Lesson

7. Instruct Students:
- Draw an oval.
- Draw two circles on top of the oval.
- Draw a long skinny oval on each side of the larger oval. Add triangles as the feet.
- Draw two long arms coming down the center of the large oval.
- Fill in the eye balls, make a mouth and VOILA!
- Make a speech bubble of the frog saying what you learned today (ie: Stay Organized!)

8. Evaluation: Raise your hand if you now think you could draw a frog in 1-2 minutes? Typically it is easier to take things one step at a time... stay organized.

9. Encourage students to take their frogs home and challenge their mothers, aunts, siblings to see if they can draw a frog in one minute. Some students even like to draw the step by step visuals on the back of their art work.

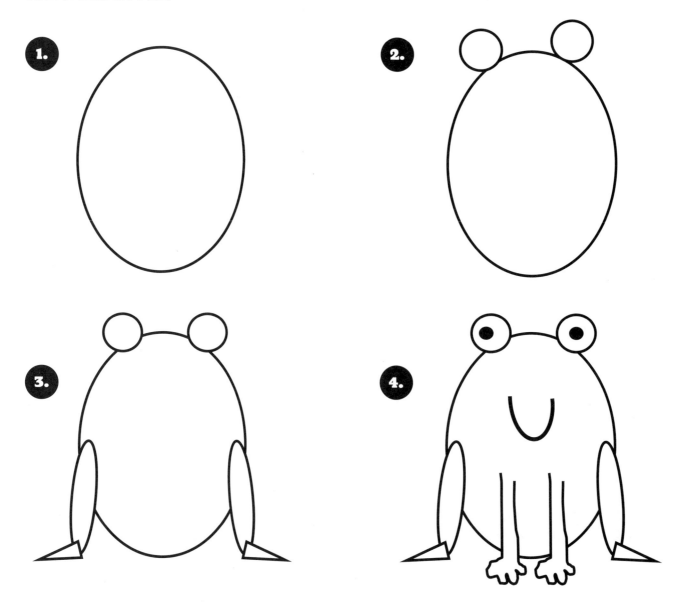

138 • ©YouthLight

Condensed Bibliotherapy List

Below are books that will correlate with the lesson ideas within this book. There is a line before each book so that you can mark where it is located, so that if you decide to use it in a lesson you know where to find it. (Personal Library, Media Center, online audiobook, Public Library, or Need to Order it).

For a short synopsis of each book, look on the literature link page within that chapter.

CAREER EXPLORATION (see pages 15-16 for synopsis)

_____ *Snowmen at Work* by Carolyn Buehner
_____ *Clothesline Clues To Jobs People Do* by Kathryn Heling
_____ *There* by Marie Louise-Fitzpatrick
_____ *Someday* by Eileen Spinelli
_____ *These Hands* by Margartet Mason
_____ *Silly Lilly in What Will I Be Today*
_____ *Sally Gets a Job* by Stephen Huneck
_____ *How to Get a Job…by Me, the Boss (How To Series)* by Sally Lloyd-Jones
_____ *A New Job for Dilly* by Rena Jones
_____ *The Night Worker* by Kate Banks
_____ *Big Plans* by Bob Shea
_____ *Whose Tools are These?* by Katz Cooper
_____ *Sid the Squid: and the Search for the Perfect Job* by David Derrick
_____ *LMNO Peas* by Keith Baker
_____ *My Name is not Isabella* by Jennifer Fosberry

WORK ETHIC (see pages 56-57 for synopsis)

_____ *Back to Front and Upside Down* by Claire Alexander
_____ *The Dot* by Peter Reynolds
_____ *Tops and Bottoms* by Janet Stevens
_____ *The Boy Who Harnessed the Wind* by William Kamkwamba and Bryan Mealer
_____ *Last to Finish: A Story About the Smartest Boy in Math Class* by Barbara Esham
_____ *Can I Have Some Money?: Max Gets It!* By Candi Sparks
_____ *Princesses are Not Quitters* by Kate Lum
_____ *Wilma Unlimited* by Kathleen Krull
_____ *Winners Never Quit* by Mia Hamm
_____ *Edgar the Eagle in Do Your Best!* By Sheila Hairston
_____ *I Will Try* by Marilyn Janovitz
_____ *Long Shot: Never Too Small to Dream Big* by Chris Paul
_____ *Pepper Parrot's Problem with Patience: A Captain No Beard Story* by Carole P. Roman

Condensed Bibliotherapy List

SELF-CONTROL (see page 76 for synopsis)

_____ *My Mouth is a Volcano* by Julia Cook

_____ *Oh No George* by Chris Haughton

_____ *Lacey Walker Non-Stop Talker* by Christianne Jones and Robert Watson

_____ *Can't Wait Willow* by Cindy Ziglar

_____ *Mrs. Gorski I have the Wiggly Fidgets* by Barbara Esham

_____ *In One Ear Out the Other* by Michael Dahl

TEAMWORK (see pages 96-97 for synopsis)

_____ *Michael's Golden Rule* by Deloris Jordan

_____ *Teamwork Isn't My Thing and I Don't Like to Share* by Julia Cook

_____ *Pumpkin Soup* by Helen Cooper

_____ *Game Day* by Tiki Barber

_____ *Joni and the Fallen Star: Helping Children Learn Teamwork* by Cindi Jett Pilon

_____ *Sophie and the Perfect Poem: Habit 6* by Sean Covey

_____ *Swimmy* by Leo Lionni

_____ *Chopsticks* by Amy Krouse Roenthal

_____ *The Best Colors* by Barbara Taff

_____ *Crayon Box that Talked* by Shane DeRolf

_____ *The Day the Crayons Quit* by Drew Daywalt

_____ *Friendship is an ART* by Julia Cook

ORGANIZATION (see page 119 for synopsis)

_____ *Lazy Daisy* by David Olson

_____ *The Messiest Desk* by Marty Kelley

_____ *Wyatt Wonder Dog Learns About Being Organized* by Lynn Watts

_____ *Messy Melinda* by Nancy Heller

_____ *The Desk Fairy* by Connie Schnoes

_____ *A Place for Everything: Habit 3 (The 7 Habits of Happy Kids)* by Sean Covey

_____ *Get Organized Without Losing It* by Janet S. Fox

_____ *Froggy Gets Dressed* by Jonathan London

_____ *Zip, Zip ... Homework* by Nancy Poydar